GET OUT OF MY BUBBLE

Get Out Of My Bubble

Introvert's Guide To Life And Avoiding People

ANUNG VILAY

Courageous Creativity

Thanks Mom for letting me be weird

Contents

Chapter 1

Introduction

I really don't like people.

I will avoid any crowd I possibly can. Even if there are people I know and like in there I will still debate whether or not to see them. Because all those people and all that noise is just draining. No matter how much fun I have, I have to figure out how much energy I want to use up for anything.

And believe me, you know many people like this. Some may be hard to spot because we've been forced to adapt. Going around talking to people they don't want to. Pretending to enjoy all the people around them. Tired of everybody's crap.

I'm only half joking with this. We are not all such downers, but some of the articles out there make us seem like it. Like we purposefully go through life making things harder and suck all the fun out of things.

I've always been the weird one. So me disappearing for days on end didn't really bother people. And my mom never had to worry about where I was half the time. I was either at dance, staying at one of 2 friends' place, the library/ bookstore, or reading in my room.

As she's always said, she loved having boring children.

Not to say I didn't go out and do stuff. Hell, every other weekend in High school I was staying at a friend's for the whole weekend. We would stay up all night watching anime, reading, and having deep discussions. All great things for my little introverted heart. We could just be reading different things in the same room for hours and not say a word to each other.

But we all still went out to the movies, walked around the mall, and a bunch of other events. Because I enjoyed doing those too. Just like I had fun at punk rock concerts. You wouldn't think an introvert would willingly go to one of those.

Bet you wouldn't think I'd also run a conference and several podcasts. Hell, my first and most popular one is what inspired this book. I know I needed to have content out in the world to draw people to my business. And I was *DONE* with blogging. It was boring and nothing about it was helping anyone.

I had listened to podcasts sporadically and a few people around me started making their own. So I decided to join a podcasting meet-up (I love me some meet-ups). Going to Women In Podcasting gave me the knowledge and courage to start my own. Which was hard at first since I hate the sound of my voice and you kind of need to listen back to what you recorded to edit.

But doing a mostly solo podcast worked well for my introverted heart. I got to talk to myself and not seem weird (or as weird). I got to talk and research about fun and sometimes funny topics. And I had another excuse to use my journals and notebooks for outlining.

Not soon after starting to do interviews. And I enjoyed it all. Actually started to get some decent listens and subscribers from it. People really liked it because I took a more humorous stance to being an introvert. Yes, I wanted to share stuff that would be helpful to use. But I wasn't going to make it psychology heavy. Which is what most podcasts about introverts were out there. And I wasn't gonna lie about some of the weird shit we do.

But depending on when and where you met me some wouldn't even know I was an introvert. Mostly because over the years I've been forced to adapt. A lot of moving, a lot of new situations.

No matter how good I get at being in new situations doesn't change me being an introvert. Some can get better on parts that are not great by society standards, but others we cannot. There will always be parts that are not up to their standards.

* * *

Getting to this book may seem weird. In 2016 I started my business and blog Courageous Creativity. Not gonna lie, the first year was rough. I wasn't 100% sure what I was doing with it or how I helped anyone. I hated writing my blog. I wasn't even interested in it, no reason anyone else should have been.

Luckily, I found some great groups to get help in. I personally know Jenna of Twin Cities Collective and she was talking about starting a podcast (called Collective Marketing Podcast, check it out). She even told me about the group

Women In Podcasting. Of course, I went to the next meeting, I love me some meet-ups.

And it was the kick in the butt I needed. Just only a few months I had my first podcast up and running. Not gonna lie, it wasn't great. But as the saying goes "done is better than perfect". I didn't wait until I got all the equipment, perfected editing, or had a marketing plan. I still don't like the sound of my voice, but I was having too much fun just making it for it to stop me. And I got better. I figured out better programs, was able to make it flow better.

It took some time, my first season was recorded on an iPad. I McGuyvered the shit out of everything. And I make mistakes. Not having backups. Having the change the name partway through because I didn't do my research enough to see if anyone had the trademark. By the time of this publication, The Introvert's Bubble will be in its 4th season. Plus 3 other podcasts and books. My first book is already out that connects to my second podcast (Living Off The Hustle, and I Don't Wanna Fit In podcast).

Of course, I was terrified to get my voice out there. Blogging was the way to go to still be separated and not be in the light. But podcasting made it so much easier to get content out and still allow for my personality to come through. And it actually worked for my personality. I work months in advance and most episodes are solo. So by the time it comes out I don't even remember enough of what I said to feel embarrassed.

But the biggest push I got was when the book Quiet by Susan Cain came out in 2012 it gave me such vindication. Showing that there are so many of us out there (plus the introduction on ambivert). That it's all a spectrum and we all can be good and bad at things. We don't all just fall into one big box of where we do and do not do.

Just like any other introvert out there we can push ourselves and grow. We can still flourish in things that we would normally do. This book is not to get you to fit in enough to get by but to know what your strengths are. To find how to use what you have to get shit down and to upgrade other parts that you want or need. But also to make your own space in the world that fits just you.

Being an introvert is a part of who we are and it permeates everything we do in big and small ways. But it does not define everything we do. We can still do and enjoy things that most would not think we would. I mean about 50% of the population sits on the introvert and ambivert spectrum so there are a lot of us out in the world, it's not just extroverts sitting in clubs or going to concerts. Yeah, society usually doesn't reward us as much as loudmouth people cause we all aren't hermits.

We don't always decline invitations out or refuse to go out in public. If you add all the stereotypes together you will see how ridiculous the picture gets. But we do not need to change who we are. I will always prefer to sit at home to read or write.

The world won't end if I do it more than some think I should. People need to mind their own business. I pay my taxes and don't commit murder. We want the same things in life as everyone else, it just can sometimes look different. And I'm not saying I have it all together. But I have tried enough things. Failed and succeeded. And I want that for you too. To create space for yourself in this world where you can be happy and whole. With all the other pieces of you, just existing.

This book is part stories and part guide. Since I've known myself to be an introvert for most of my life I've had a lot of time to reflect on it. But also keep it in mind for a lot of what I went through in life. For most, it played a part in what I did or felt. It colors all my interactions in the world. Plus, some of this shit is funny and I know y'all would find it funny. All I've ever wanted to do was guide and entertain at the same time.

So buckle up cause I'm going to push the boundaries of what you thought was possible for your mindset. Then give you practical steps for most situations in life.

Chapter 2

Fact and Fiction

There has been a big push to understand ourselves more, but in a more accepting way. Not trying to fit everyone in a box or change so everyone is the same. There have been huge bounds in research and I have been nerding out reading it all.

But there is still a lot of misinformation out there. Mostly from people making the introvert out to be very one dimensional or confusing them for other things, mostly pertaining to mental health. There is actually nothing wrong with being an introvert. We are not being difficult or trying to be different. Other peoples' opinions are none of our business. We do not have to deny parts of ourselves just to make them comfortable.

Screw that shit.

You'd think now with the internet people would be able to do a little search just to understand others. Google that shit if you are confused. If my dad can look things up, even though his English isn't great and his spelling is worse than mine, everyone else can.

The Short and Simple

Fundamentally, an introvert is someone who gains energy from doing things alone or in very small groups. They lose energy in big gatherings, loudspeaker places, and general things that have no depth to them. Now, this doesn't make them bad or less fun. They can participate in all the same things as an extrovert, but they just don't gain energy from them.

We need our solitude to recharge. This can be watching a movie, reading, writing, listening to music, having deep discussions with a friend, and really anything that we can do alone for a long period of time. And it doesn't have to be relaxing and easy to do this. Doing some intensive work or research for hours can rev you up.

Sadly, there are still a lot of misconceptions out there about us. Mostly because in America we are more of an extroverted society. Being boisterous, confident, loud, and always working well with others is encouraged. And instead of adapting to be helpful and accepting of others, what "most" people will do is try to change us to make things easier for them. Yes, some don't know they are doing this. Most of us are not trained psychologists.

With more people being more accepting of others in all ways I thought I'd just throw us in there. It really isn't hard, especially since we're about 50% of the population.

Surprising huh?

There is actually research out there that says that there are many of us out there. For so long it was believed that the numbers were more in the 20% range. But really, we like to be left alone and not talk to strangers so I can see how people missed some of us.

But there are some other things that are specifically attributed to us that have nothing to do with being an introverts

Anti-social

Just because we don't always want to go out all the time does not make us anti-social. Yeah, we can decline more often than others when they ask for us to do specific things. Cause, I'm always going to decline to go to your kid's play date. One because it's weird you invited me because I have no kids. Two, I cannot handle all the loudness of children. That is not a situation that I find any joy in.

We seem to get more flack for declining even though we can be as busy as anyone else. You may also only be inviting us to big gatherings or to places that are really loud. Or people get upset because you don't stay as long. Mostly because you have run out of energy. You make sure you say your goodbyes, remind people that you did have a good time and leave because you are DONE.

Never Talk

It's kind of hard to get a word in when people won't shut up.

That's only partially true. Sometimes we are just listening. Shocker, not enough people actually do that. We are really good listeners. We also could have nothing to say. We may not know much about the topic so don't have anything to add. Or we could be bored with it and hope you will move on. Not every conversation needs all your energy in it.

We also take more time to process. This can be in meetings or just regular conversations. Sometimes we need time to gather our thoughts to say something. It doesn't make us stupid, but it can suck when the conversation moves on before we can say anything.

We're Lonely

Craving solitude and being lonely are two different things. So no, we don't need you to 'rescue' us from our lonely world. We do know how to get out. We will text you. Of course, we do like being invited if you have something going on. But not out of pity.

There is such a stigma for anyone actually wanting to be alone. That there's something wrong with us. Why wouldn't we want to hang with our friends? Why can't we talk to our family every day? We're just hiding it and need to be rescued.

Shy

Being shy and introverted are two different things, again. A shy person doesn't want to be alone but is uncomfortable and afraid to interact with others. You can outgrow, learn to overcome, or go to therapy for shyness. You don't 'get over' being an introvert.

There are other things that I could go into, but you get the drift. We are not rude, depressed, have low self-esteem, are weird, or hate people. Anyone can have those things for any reason, but they are not associated with introversion exclusively. There are a lot of other reasons why I'm weird which have nothing to do with that. And believe me, that seems normal compared to the real things.

We are all complex beings. Nothing about us fits into little, simple boxes.

Some Things We Are

Just to make you have a better picture of what introverts are here are some good examples. But as with everything with humanity we are a variety. No specific thing really defines us to the point that it's true for everyone. But there are some things that fit most of us. And it's a good start to remembering for yourself and to point out to others.

Thinking Things Through

Yes, this can be bad sometimes when we're going in circles about things. But we are rarely unprepared. We will go deep into things and know whatever we can about any given topic. This can just be about things we enjoy working on and projects. When we work on anything we will get it all done and figure out all the things that could be wrong.

This doesn't say that we are not spontaneous but we like to see all sides for most situations. I still took a risk with starting a business and learned every possible thing I could upfront. I like to know the rules and conventions with a group/situation as much as I can. Mostly if I break a rule or am rude you will know that I did it on purpose.

Asking Questions

It can be hard to talk up sometimes but when it really counts we will ask questions when needed. And sometimes it's what is really needed when people get carried away with something and not actually figuring out the important stuff.

We would rather not have small talk so will try to inject questions into conversations. If I have to have another interaction where I tell the 18th person what I do for work I might scream (only on the inside and find a private room). I will ask what you are working on, what you love about your work, and any funny stories you have. If we're gonna talk we are gonna interact. If I'm going to talk to someone I want to actually remember the conversation.

Damn Good At Listening

You know the one thing people need more of? People who listen. Too many out there listen just to respond and not to actually engage. Our friends and family need it. People at work need it. We are the ones listening. Hell, we listen when people don't realize we are. I'm not above eavesdropping.

We are usually better at considering the thoughts, feelings, and ideas of others. A good listener tries to stay neutral while trying to understand. We also try not to jump to conclusions before hearing everything. We can do that mostly with ourselves. We are also good at seeing everything that's being said in subtleties and body language. This feeds into the point above; by listening we can ask better questions.

Not Taking Any Of Your Shit

I'm not saying that we all are confrontational but that we will have no problem sometimes just ghosting people. We feel no remorse (some can have shame) in not talking to certain people because of what they say, how they make us feel, or the lack of respect they have for others. So many of us have no problem sliding away from people and generally avoid them.

Though we are made to feel that how we are and want to not do some things is wrong and inconvenient to others. But sooner or later we start to get comfortable with ourselves and see we are not a problem. And we get really tired of all the noise out there. So for our own mental health, we just don't allow people's shit sometimes.

Chapter 3

Recharging

Everyone needs to recharge. It's the basis of self-care which should not be skipped. For some people, after a long hard day at work, they want to unwind at happy hour with some friends. That does not sound relaxing to me, at all. Now that doesn't mean I wouldn't find it fun, that after a stressful day that the idea would not be even a possibility.

But in this go go go world it can be hard to get the time to do what we need. We have work trying to get us to work outside of work, friends and family, and even things we want to do outside. All those take up time. And too many times we feel pressured and guilted to spend all our time with people.

We can't change who or what we are. No matter how much we may enjoy an activity and the people we do it with, it still drains our energy. The main way we get our energy back is with solitude. And that can be done in many different ways. Usually doing it solo and alone with our thoughts.

Reading

This is an easy one. Most people picture an introvert as someone with their nose in a book. But it's not always easy to do. Yeah, technically you open a book and put your eyes on the page. But sometimes you are not in the mood for something for it to be recharging.

Doing this a lot is not anti-social in any way. It's, for many, a go-to for recharging. I almost always have a book on me for when things get boring. Luckily now ebooks are more available so I always have something on hand. There are times when you're with someone and they have to run an errand that might take a while. I have no problem sitting in a car reading for 30 minutes. I promise you I will not be bored.

I have brought one to weddings and big family parties. Especially when I was younger and had to wait to leave until my parent(s) were ready to go. So instead of sitting there bored with a bunch of strangers, I'll find a quiet spot to read. I'm not bothering anyone and the person can enjoy themself longer.

I have times where I can read a fiction book if my life depended on it. It could even be from one of my favorite authors, that I know I'm going to love. But I can't get into it. Maybe you want something light. A guaranteed happy ending. Something that will really make you think. Or something that will really get you thinking.

Sometimes the reading isn't the most important part, but what you get out of it. At the time of writing this chapter, I'm in a nonfiction phase. But something that's more inspirational. Most to help boost my creativity and loosen more ideas to get me writing. But in the editing stage of any writing, I want nothing that will make me think. Reading an article might even annoy me. Other times I've actually read some medical journals (I have a thing for reading scientific and medical research sometimes) because that interests me. For other people that may be anxiety-inducing.

I really don't think I need to explain to you that it lowers stress. Unless it's a character that does something so stupid you get second-hand embarrassment and want to throw the book. But you still enjoy it. There are a few other good reasons to read, ones I never thought of.

Fiction Increases Empathy and Social Intelligence:

- We become comfortable with ambiguity
- We can make better decisions
- We get better at communicating

Who would have thought a solitary activity would make me better at speaking? Not to say it will get rid of any anxiety. Not only do we get to see all the ways people can communicate, but we can see how it can get awkward. Possibly desensitizing us to some situations.

The more we read, the more words we are exposed to. Having more knowledge also makes it easier to talk about things. We can also see all the possibilities to make a decision. Not what we feel or what others believe to be right. Sometimes in fiction, not everything is resolved. Pieces are left out, like in life which prepares us for it in life in small ways.

Nap

When all else fails, take a nap.

I always feel like naps are our bodies turning us off and on. Just a quick reset to get things moving again. They don't even need to be long to get some great benefits. And there are 5 types of naps according to The Sleep Foundation:

- Recovery Nap: Sleep deprivation and to compensate for sleep loss.
- Prophylactic Nap: Taken in preparation for sleep loss.
- Appetitive Nap: Appetitive naps are taken for the enjoyment of napping.
- Fulfillment Nap: Children have a greater need for sleep than adults.
- Essential Nap: When you are sick, you have a greater need for sleep.

And depending on which kind you do depends on the length of nap you take. For an Essential you sleep as long as you need to help with healing. While some of the others are more to take to help with deprivation (whether before or after). So you do not need to nap as long as what sleep you missed, but just enough to be functional.

These are a little harder to work into your life. Some days you don't or even want to take a nap. You may have days where you really do not have the time. But we all have some time to allow this sometimes in a week.

Daydream

This is honestly my favorite thing to do. We all have done it. Imagining the first day of school, your first date, or getting transported to another world to topple an empire. (Just me?) Either way, in moments of quiet we allow ourselves to dream of something big.

And you can't do this wrong. It can be serious or whimsical. You can even play out something that will be happening in the future. Visualization falls into this to help prepare yourself or to ease anxiety. But in the end, it gives your mind a break from the immediate reality.

Because not focusing on things will actually help you focus later. Research even says that people who daydream more are more likely to get their goals they fantasized about. It also improves your creativity. So much of the major innovations in the world came from people's imagination and being allowed to dream of something new and better.

Ever daydreamed during a turbulent time and wanted to get your mind off things? You make up a story and try to relax, but pieces on your life filter in some. But after going through you come up with an idea or uncover a truth. Releasing the stress and letting your mind roam allows it to uncover things you were not able to. You can think of this as your mind working through things, or your intuition and inner truth being allowed out.

Meditation

We all know meditation is so good for us. You can't turn around without getting hit with a news report or blog post touting it. Which isn't bad, but hearing about it all the time can get a person to not try it. The thing is, you don't have to be monk-like and spend an hour doing it every day to get the benefits.

What most people don't realize is that the end part of most yoga classes is a kind of meditation. Even for some of the short classes. The corpse pose where you lay down and relax has the same benefits. They actually tell you to clear your mind and release any thoughts that come out. It works better for me because I've gotten a good workout and stretch just before.

Another option is to do a walking meditation. There are actual guide walking meditations you can listen to while you do it. But you can also do it in silence, whether around your neighborhood or in nature. Of course, make sure you do this someplace where you can be safe since you will not be vigilant about your surroundings.

Some of the other really good benefits that are specific to introverts are:

- It can keep our over-thinking and perfectionism in check
- Reconnect with yourself
- Be in the present more
- It can help with your fight or flight response

Watching TV/Movies/Videos

I know there's a lot out there that say that we watch too much TV and stare at our screens all the time. But sometimes you want to get lost in a story or just veg out with something mind-numbing. It still accomplishes the same thing. Letting you not think.

And I don't care that doing this can "melt your brain". Not everything we do needs to enhance us or better our lives. Sometimes you just want all the noise around you and inside to just shut up. If you enjoy it and you don't neglect important things then people can bugger off.

A 2012 study out of the University of Buffalo found that people who watch TV, especially ones that are familiar, are able to stay on top of their self-control better than those who don't watch lots of TV. According to another, watching nature shows makes people feel more generous and energetic. Plus it can help lower blood pressure and relieve stress.

Hobbies

Honestly, a lot of what's already talked about here can all be considered a hobby. It's something to do in your free time for fun and to relax. But I don't mean relax and it's all calm and mellow. More that it doesn't completely stress you out and you actually enjoy it even if it's exhausting. I mean, I'm all for being lazy when I can but sometimes what's fun isn't always easy.

Now, I love writing but it can be a little stressful trying to make a scene work or when I can't remember a freaking word. Or when I throw pottery on a wheel its very satisfying to create something, but it's tiring on the arms and my back is usually killing me in the end. But I get immersed in it so much that I get out of my head. It may not be relaxing which makes it enjoyable.

There is no real outcome that you have to get out of them. Yeah, you can get satisfaction from creating something and getting to the goal. But the act itself lets you not think about anything else, and ignore anybody around you. I don't even need to go over how it receives stress, all these things do. But it will take your mind off of anything, which in turn can give you the space to see it differently. It can challenge you in a less pressured way that will let you work through it better.

And drinking wine with your friends is not a hobby. A hobby is going to all the regions to make wine and learning all the different ways they make it and how different ingredients can change the taste. And drink it all. It's not a hobby to just watch the baseball game at home alone. It's a hobby when you go to all the home games of your favorite teacher, have a fantasy league, and are in a team that plays for fun.

Now I love anime, but watching it doesn't give me much. It's finding the manga and discussing the differences between the two. Going to conventions to see my favorite artist. Creating costumes for cosplay. Someday planning a trip to Japan to immerse myself in the culture (respectfully). It needs to take you out of yourself, even for a short time. But also have some physical activity to it. Whether it's going to someone's house to debate it, or carrying the whole series from the bookstore.

Listening To Music

There are two ways to go about this. The one most will think about is to listen to music to relax. This can be the classic round of soft, soothing music. Or even listening to a playlist of your favorite songs. The main point is to relax. I've even made playlists to daydream to.

But also, introverts are really not known for liking loud music. Not in our homes, not at parties. We want to be able to still think. And for something too loud can be agitating. Let alone when you're out and can't talk to someone.

Anyone else actually turn down the music in their car when they are lost or looking for a street?

But there are times when we will blast it. When we are really going through something or running on high emotions. We don't want to have to think. Throw on a song about horrible relationships, cheating, or just lying people in general. You just want to scream and cry with it. It may also be the beat or feeling you get that you want to wash over you.

I mean, I grew up in a time when punk rock and emo music was at their height. So I got a lot of angst shit.

And it doesn't have to be about anything negative. You may have gotten great news and am happy and excited. So you crank that shit up and let all the joy out. Because some of what helps for recharging and releasing some of what has built up in us.

Hang With A Friend

This may seem counter-productive. We are not known to get energy from people. But if you have a really good friend that you can be 100% with, that's great. And the thing is, you don't even have to do stuff together or really talk. Watch a movie together. Hell, I've had times where we actually just hung out reading in the same room. Barely said anything for hours. But we would take breaks to talk and eat.

The point is it's with a friend that gets you. There isn't anything to put on. Nothing has to be presentable. Not your home or yourself. You just hang and not worry about judgment. But also because this friend will be a sounding board.

They will be on your side and help you work on any problem. But they will also call you out on your shit.

Having Companionship and Acceptance Is What Helps.

To so many, the thought of doing something with another person doesn't seem to fit the purpose of recharging. It only works with some situations and cannot be done every time. This is not a push to try and make you more extroverted.

This isn't just hanging with any friend. This is that one (or two) that gets you. No side looks about what you eat. No sighing when you talk about something you enjoy again. The energy just works together. No, you may not have a person like this yet. So don't feel pressured to do this if it's not what you need.

Journal

Sometimes you just want to get something out of your head, but you don't really want to talk about it. Journaling is a great way to not keep it all in.

Reduces Stress

Sometimes you just don't want to talk to someone when you have a problem. It could be because you don't have anyone that would understand it that you just want to work on it on your own for now. But keeping things bottled up is not good for you. And this is a good way to get it out.

It also releases stress in making you really think through whatever's on your mind. You get more details down on top of all the emotions going on. Sometimes uncovering things you haven't noticed before.

Improves Memory

Going over details, even after the fact, helps you to remember. Especially if you write it out soon after things happen. I like to make sure I not only give the details but what I was feeling. The details are important so no one can try to manipulate you into believing what you know to be true. Plus they can't make you feel like it wasn't that bad or to let them do it again.

The emotions are just as important. You need to remember how something makes you feel so you can know to avoid it or replicate it. If someone makes you feel like crap and you need to remember how their presence makes you feel so that you don't allow them to repeat it.

Boosts Your Mood

Getting the chance to let things out will not let it fester inside of you. Sometimes you don't have someone to talk about a certain thing. Or it will be days before someone will be available. So instead of leaving it in you can work your own way through it

Improves Immune Function

One study shows that those who journaled while getting a series of the Hepatitis vaccine had no side effects. They also had higher antibodies up to 2 months after the last shot. Journaling works on two levels, our feelings and thinking. Being able to express our feelings and organize our thoughts can distance us from what is bothering us.

Strengthens You Emotional Connection

It makes you more mindful and helps you remain in the present. Releasing any bottled up emoticons can help you regulate them. Letting you evaluate them so they don't swing to extremes without you being able to stop them. Being able to know your own emotions, how you react, and why will help with your own confidence. Confident that your emotions will not take over or hurt others.

Chapter 4

Being Yourself

Being yourself is never an easy thing. Things get lost in the shuffle of life and to-do lists. You have other obligations that always seem to push their way forward. Things that don't need "you" are an individual, but you as a worker "doing".

Me going to the grocery store takes no personality. Even at work, you're there, but you need to be slightly different to fit into what you are doing. Enough of us that have worked with people have a "customer service" voice. A lot of us fake who we are in the world. To get things done or to even be taken seriously.

But it is exhausting. Always having to be "on".

We are constantly pushed out of our comfort zones to make life "easier" for others. Being pushed extra to talk to people, get out of our solitude. All in the name of what's best for us. But it isn't always.

I've moved over 10 times by the time I graduated high school. It was always tough making new friends. Always being the new kid. I had to put on a persona to not be constantly alone. I got really good at making friends in school. Just not great at keeping them. So when I got into high school it was a little harder.

Finding Who You Are

In all the time we grow up we are finding pieces of ourselves. The things we like to do, food we don't like eating, and any kind of quirks. But we also are learning things. Some useful, like learning to read and write to critical thinking. Other things may not be great. Such as being able to tell someone is angry so you can be sure to be quieter to not upset them more. Or always being the mediator for everyone's problems.

So much of what is us is what we pick up from our lives and environment. Some to help us grow and hopefully thrive, but some things are just so we can survive. Things in your culture that you grew up with. The different dynamics in your family. Even the little things we pick up in our friend's group.

But all along, you are finding pieces of yourself.

For the most part, we don't really think about it all as we're growing up. Puberty can be a bitch and not exactly conducive to deep, introspective thinking. But pieces get revealed. You try things out with friends. Like different music, sports, books, hobbies, and everything else in-between. And as the hormones calm down you get to notice more things you don't like. Honestly, your 20s are the time to explore. Your teens are practically finding all your pieces together while the 20s are how they fit together. Kind of like putting together some furniture or electronics but look at the instructions and warnings later.

There are some important questions to ask yourself that's specific to being an introvert. Nothing too deep, but knowing the answers can help you make choices that will keep you happier.

- What introverted things do you not enjoy?
- What extroverted things do you like to do?
- what specific things drain you? How long do you need to recharge from them?

Here are some other non-introvert questions to work through, and these are deep:

- What are 5-10 traits that I feel define me?
- How do others perceive me?
- What roles do I place in my family and friends' groups?
- What are some of my strengths and weaknesses?
- What are some of my core values?

At a basic level, knowing who you are just makes you happier. You know your likes and dislikes. You can work on doing of your likes and learn from why you dislike other things. But it's also about self-awareness, which in turn increases your emotional intelligence. Which can help you intensify and manage your feelings, so as not to repress them or get lost in them. You know what your standards are and will focus more on them than trying to live to others.

It All Connects

Depending on how you see your introversion depends on how you feel about this. Its not so defining that it chocks you, not allowing any free will. But it is part of your foundation and will never go away. Parts can change, some, but you will never "get better". One, because there's nothing wrong with you. Two, there's only so much you can change.

For some, not being able to change can seem like a horrible thing. But I'm happy about it. I never prescribed to the idea that you need to fix all your weaknesses. Yes, you should work on them some so they are not a detriment to your life. I'd rather spend time working on my strengths and getting others to make up for my shortcomings. This means more having someone who is better at talking to strangers and you remembering to send a thank you card.

Being an introvert is just a part of who you are. Yes, I identify as one and it does color a lot of what I do in life but it doesn't rule me completely. I may still go to a loud bar to hang with friends, hate the music, but still enjoy myself. Still exhausted but had fun.

But it all connects to everything about you. I'm always going to be a dog person. Me being an introvert constantly wars with going up to people to ask if I can pet their dog. But also being a creative, I created a shirt saying "Please let me pet your dog". So sometimes I can go up to people and just point at the shirt. Still being polite to ask but skipping the step to needing to talk.

I love taking personality quizzes. Some are ridiculous, but others are actually really good. I just love learning about myself. Now I know some may think most of these are useless and mean nothing. That's your opinion but doesn't give you the right to shit on other's stuff.

I'm all woo woo and believe in astrology. Being a Capricorn fits me to a tee. But it doesn't dictate my whole life, just influences it. It doesn't mean I'm heartless and only care about money. Same as saying "sorry I'm late, I'm an Aquarius". No Susan, you just don't respect anyone's time.

I've even done several episodes talking about this. Partially because I just like discussing them and also to show people how one trait can make it easy for me to talk with a bunch of strangers at a conference, but another wanting to run across traffic to get away.

- Sun sign Capricorn, Moon sign Leo
- Myers-Briggs INTJ
- Love Language Quality Time
- 4 Tendencies Rebel
- Enneagram 9
- Human Design Generator

There are other things I can add, but these are the ones that I think about the most in life. Knowing what pizza topping I am will not change anyone's opinion of me. Though some have some strong feelings about pineapple.

The Myers-Briggs is an easy one to start with. The "I" in it stands for Introvert. The rest of the traits stand for Intuitive, Thinking, and Judging. They are usually known as the tacticians love perfecting the details of life, applying creativity and rationality to everything they do. Their inner world is often a private, complex one.

The thing about this is that fits very well with my Tendency type. Neither type likes others having authority over them. We like to go our own way, making our own discoveries instead of relying on others to always know. We do not like being told what to do.

Which also connects to my Human Design as a Generator. We can find the answers we need within ourselves. Because our authority, or inner truth, is in our sacral center. Other people's plans have nothing to do with us.

Having To Lie

I've actually had someone be very adamant that introverts lie a lot and are very good at it. Now, this is the only person who I've ever heard this from but it did get me thinking. Us being seen as so "different" and forced to do things to fit in, some might think of that as lying.

There are times we will do things or pretend to be someone else to avoid the worst of a situation. Pretending you don't speak English? Not look at someone so they can not notice them waving at you? Money Mindset Coach Dennis Duffield-Thomas* had a made-up assistant (when before she couldn't afford one) that would have no problem enforcing boundaries and being the bad cop. Or when two colleagues exchange emails to work with clients and the male gets treated with more respect and questioned less. Even if they are equal in their jobs and skills, or even the female is higher.

There have been plenty of other times when we have had to lie just to be left alone to do our own thing or for others to stop harassing us. Who hasn't walked around with headphones on so people won't talk to you? Or just disappeared from a party for a bit, to either hide outside or a room, and just say to people you were moving around and

that's why they didn't see you? What about telling someone you're busy because you just don't have the energy to
hang but they will get upset if you tell the truth?

Yeah, we may be not telling the whole truth all the
time but we mostly do it because people get upset with us
for not being accommodating. Or that we are supposed to
change parts of ourselves to make them more comfortable.

Move in the world the way you need to. I'm not gonna
judge.

Letting Yourself In

You never find all you who you are in one go. It's a
constant exploration that starts early and only slows down
when you're a lot older. But that is only half the battle. The
other half is accepting what you find. You can never really
thrive in life if you're constantly fighting against what you
are fundamentally. Which sucks since so much is thrown
at us telling us there's always something wrong. We're too
old, too young. Too smart, think too highly of ourselves.
Too quiet, yet we need to let the people who "know" what
they're saying talk.

It's hard enough to accept who you are will all the crap
society throws at you. What you can and cannot do because
of your gender, getting married, having kids, don't com-
plain, and a million other things.

It can seem impossible sometimes to just accept a lot of
the pieces of you that don't quite fit with the rest of the
world. But you will never be truly happy if you don't allow
the pieces that cannot be changed. We will never not need
to recharge after big gatherings. We will never not need
space to ourselves.

You will need to allow these parts and not be angry, frustrated, or discouraged about them. There really needs to be no emotion about it. It just is and you can live with it. No one is perfect. So we all need to work around things that just don't work for a situation. It doesn't make you difficult or a bad person. Just something different and personal. And it's not like you are making anyone's life more difficult for it.

And we need to stop worrying about how others see and judge us. Some will never understand and are set in their ways. They also have their own limiting beliefs that they are working through. If you're not hurting anyone then it's no ones' business.

Chapter 5

Setting And Protecting Boundaries

Not gonna lie, this is going to be a touchy section. Partially because you're going to have to dig deep to work through this and it's going to hurt to establish these boundaries. You're going to have to examine a lot of things in your life. Why you do some things. Why you don't other things. Then figure out how you want to live your life and how you want to be treated.

Then you will need to set up said boundaries. Which the hard part will not be you but everyone else running up against it. Most people will in the beginning, which isn't bad, since it's not how you operated before. So you will have to tell them about it. Some it will take some time for them you get the picture. What will be hard for you is staying firm with them.

Others will actively fight against it. Some not wanting things to change because of fear. But too many because they don't want to lose the benefits they got for you not having the boundary.

Boundaries are you setting up how you want to be treated. The limitations on who can in certain spaces and for how long with you. Having them is for your own good. You are not being selfish for having any. They help boost your self-esteem, let you not waste energy, and give you more independence and agency. It's also not about controlling people, but yourself. It is what you will do in response to a situation.

They also give you the space to make yourself a priority. They are also for your safety. You can see better when someone in your life is becoming unsafe. Or you can finally see how someone who you've known forever is actually not good for you. Sadly, it happens a lot with family members. But because you've lived with the treatment your whole life you don't see anything wrong with it. It's something called "the fog"* where you don't quite see all the details. But you can sense something is off and you feel bad. There's just not enough for you to put your finger on it because you can't see the whole picture.

Examples of where we can set boundaries:

- personal space
- Time and energy
- stuff and possessions
- emotions and thoughts
- Sexuality
- culture, religion, and ethics

Determine What Boundaries You Need

Now for the actual part where you do something. But everything before is important and you need to understand these to have a good foundation. Going in without a good base is a disaster waiting to happen.

There are two questions that I always ask to get me started on creating a boundary. They are simple, but really can get you emotional:

- what rights do you have?
- what are your wants and needs?

The first question you can take literally or what you believe you deserve. The first can be about the law or what you are allowed to do. Say if you have joint custody of kids or you're renting property. The other side can be if you are living with other people. Or even visiting your parents' house. You can't just completely go no-contact with your ex if there's a court order that you have to drop off the kids to each other. Or if you both have to agree on decisions pertaining to your kids. If you live with other people you can't reasonably expect quiet all the time you are home.

Of course, there are ways to get around most things. You may not always like them but you need to keep all your options open. With having to interact with an abusive ex, make sure you always have someone with you when they are around. If it's people in the same house you may have to get passive-aggressive and disrupt things they enjoy to get them to realize things are a problem. (Of course, I do not advocate being a dick, much, this is after you have tried to discuss the problem and have been ignored over and over.)

I have a really good example. I studied abroad in Ireland for a school year. Roomed with two Irish guys, an Irish girl, a Chinese guy, and me. The Irish boys did not clean, at all. They always expected someone else to do the dishes. Got to the point they would leave them so long things grew on them. The rest of us talk to them over and over for over a month. We had to keep a set of dishes in our rooms just so we could have clean things to eat on.

One weekend I finally snapped. Almost every weekend they would go home, mostly to have their moms do their laundry. They cooked and left a sink full of disgusting dishes again. They always left their rooms unlocked. So I took the dishes and spread them all over their beds. I made sure it was smeared on their sheets. The other flatmates actually stood at the doors, watching in disbelief but kind of gleeful.

When they got back a bunch of us had a few friends over, just waiting in the living room. They were talking and laughing, got into their rooms, and dead silence. A few minutes later they come in carrying the dishes. They don't really look at us, say hi, and go straight to the kitchen sink. They avoided us for the rest of the day, but were fine after that. They got some shit from their friends since no one could not tell what I did. But they always did their dishes within 24 hours after that.

The second question can take a little longer to work through. What are your wants and needs to live a happy and content life? What things are more important than others. One of mine is that I don't like to be touched, especially by people I don't know. While having people call me doesn't really bother me. Some of my quiet time needs to be completely alone, others can be fine as long as people don't interact with them.

How do you want people to interact with you? What does respect look like to you? What is actually funny to you or constitutes as a joke? What is offensive? Really figure out how you want to live your life and how you want to feel with the people around you.

Once you got these down then you need to see how they apply to everyone in your life. Everyone will have that boundary but will have variations and be enforced differently. But they will all have to be told one way or another what your boundaries are.

Which can feel really awkward, especially to people you've known for a really long time. And this doesn't mean you need to blast it all over the world once you have the boundary. That would be exhausting. Just when said boundary is being pushed, then you can bring it up with the person. Right as it's happening. Mostly so they have a glaringly obvious example of what not to do. This doesn't need to be all confrontational either. Just say it as a simple statement with as little emotion as you can. Then if you can move on.

Now, if these people are actually decent, they will just move on. Or they may ask a few clarifying questions. Which is perfectly fine. Most people just want to be sure they understand and want more details on said boundary. What is not ok is when they question you. They may get offended, make you seem like you are being difficult, and all over gaslight you.

Gaslighting is a form of psychological manipulation in which a person or a group covertly sows seeds of doubt in a targeted individual or group, making them question their own memory, perception, or judgment. It may evoke changes in them such as cognitive dissonance or low self-esteem, rendering the victim additionally dependent on the gaslighter for emotional support and validation. Using denial, misdirection, contradiction, and misinformation, gaslighting involves attempts to destabilize the victim and delegitimize the victim's beliefs.

You Can't Avoid This

It may be a default reaction for us but these types of things cannot be avoided. You're not giving yourself the chance to not be hurt. You're not giving the people in your life who care about you the option to be better. And you are giving the bullies and manipulators a free pass. Even though the first two are very important, I'll be damned if I make things easier for horrible people. But choose what drives you to do better for yourself.

We want to avoid conflict whenever we can. By staying silent, not rocking the boat, ignoring, or just running away. Either way, you're going to feel like shit. But wouldn't you rather feel it because you demanded to have your choices, time, and physical space respected? That you don't have to walk on eggshells around other people because of how they will react to anything? That you don't have to feel tired and ashamed for anything you do?

You need to be ok with people getting offended or hurt by these boundaries. Because too many will see it as control, but it's not your job to make others comfortable at your own expense. You need to not stop because people will think you are not nice for having them. Nice people make things easy for others. They make others comfortable. This gets pushed a lot on children, especially girls. Good children have manners and respect adults. Good girls are not mean and are not loud. But when does that stop? Not when you're, a teenager or a young adult. It's not suppose to stop because that's what they want from you.

They Will Be Different For Each Person

Each person will have different boundaries they will push on. Some will just need to be told what they are and they will actually work on it to not push you. But other times you will have people who will not like the change. With the friend, you may just have to give a small reminder. For the person who won't respect it, you will have to be more abrupt.

You may have to call them out since being embarrassed would be a horrible thing to them. Other times it may be a punishment or you will not talk to them for a period of time. Now, this is not a tallying of how good or bad they are. And not in the sense of punishing that you are better than them and everything you say must be obeyed. That is sliding into narcissistic territory.

Also, some people you will not need to have the boundary with. One of mine is that if we have not been talking already that evening, I don't want to be called or messaged at night. I go to bed and wake up early. But I have some friends that know and respect this and would only call if it was an emergency and I would rather know and be able to help than them not call me. Other people cannot understand that something that is important to them does not necessitate an emergency to me.

They Need To Be Flexible

Your boundaries need to strong but not stringent. They will not be set in stone because each situation may call for a little different enforcement. Not allowing your mom to tell you your path is wrong will be handled differently than your sister. Mostly because one does it out of worry and the other out of a sense of superiority. We're not going to get into the why's of these things, if you really need an explanation you need to ask them or get a therapist.

Protect Them

This leads to how to protect your boundaries. Because there will always be people who don't want you to have them. They benefited from you not having them. Let me said this loud and clear. There is *nothing* wrong with having boundaries. You are not selfish in any way and it is your own mental health.

Standing strong for them will be hard in the beginning. It will take a while to shine up your spine and be comfortable making others uncomfortable. Because many will feel called out no matter how nice or private you tell them or remind them. Some will act like you kicked a dog, spit on a baby, and wiped your ass on an American flag all at the same time. And they will confront you. Which is not an introvert's strong suit.

You may have to do things that others think are rude. If you're on the phone you may have to tell them you will not talk to them if they are like this and hang up. Do not pick up when they call back. Which they will. They do not want to lose any control they think they have. You may have to tell others what happened so they can't lie and change what happened.

Not saying you have to blast this on Facebook. Say this was a parent getting angry. So you would need to talk to your significant other and a sister. Those who are closest to you and the parent. And who knows about the situation, how you've been treated, and respect of your boundaries.

- Other examples are one aunt who texts inappropriate messages will be fine and remember you boundary when you do not reply to said messages. While a mother (or MIL) will have to be told several times and consequences be given. Like not talking to them on the phone or refusing to be anywhere alone with them. All the way to going completely no contact.
- Either way there should always be consequences to people pushing and disregarding your boundaries. The main one being access to you; your time and your presence. They get to talk to you less. You will not be telling them any important news in your life. You (and your family) will not be showing up to any birthday parties.
- This will suck because you will lose some people in your life. Which as an introvert, we don't that many of. But these will be only in your life to use you, abuse, control, and manipulate you. You don't need that. And even though it will hurt and you will feel lonely things will be so much better after they're gone.

Right after college, I did a big purge. Got rid of a lot of people I thought were friends, but were more than acquaintances and less than friends. They were more a part of another friend's group. I always felt like I had to chase them to ever hang out. Once I threw that trash out (and wallowed a bit) I found other people to have fun with. Others who were up to trying new things and were supportive of all the things I wanted to try. It may be small, but this group I trust so much more.

Respecting Others

Having others respecting our boundaries is great, but it's also healthy to do this for the people around you. Really pay attention when others tell you not to say something or pull away when you do something. They may not feel strong enough or were not allowed to set boundaries or enforce any. Just because they do not do this does not mean you cannot see it or even ask. Show them that they have a safe space with you.

I may not be great with kids, it's a mutual dislike, but I will still listen to them and give them time to open up. And the older they get the more they like me. I never ask for a hug and will ask if they can give me a high five or just a wave. Mostly because I wish I was given that option as a child. I'm not a touchy person and hugs should be reserved for people you know and like. I literally have all my friends' and cousins' kids starting to like me more now because I don't talk down to them or make them do things they are uncomfortable with. Which shocks the shit out of everybody.

Going Low or No Contact

If any of you have ever been on Reddit you will know these two terms. Pretty much means when a toxic person refuses to change and tries to create more drama you need to remove yourself from the situation. Going Low Contact is setting very strict boundaries. From how much time you spend with them, when and where you talk, to what information they are allowed to have.

These are for people who generally do not try to be hurtful and actually care about you but are ignorant (sometimes willfully) about how and why their actions are unacceptable. It can be a person who is always the last to be told things. It could because they can never keep it a secret and has to tell everyone and their cat your news. Or that they will discuss your personal stuff with anyone. Sometimes to "understand" better but usually because they want others to take their side on some perceived disagreement.

Going No Contact is a last resort but one I wish more people used. These are for the people who absolutely do not care for your needs. Everything is about them, you should cater to them, and any deviation makes you a horrible person. This can be from a parent, partner, friend, mentor, or even a child. Mostly stemming from all the many forms of abuse out there.

And it will be hard to go No Contact. You, being a good person, will feel guilty. You have been manipulated into thinking you overreact and are over-sensitive. Which you are not. You are reacting to your mistreatment and deserve better.

On top of all that you will get guilt from people around you. Others who don't want to rock the boat. People who are angry with you won't keep up and allow you to be abused along with them. Those who don't know the full truth. Other toxic people who love drama. And the granddaddy of them all "but they're *family*".

Don't get me started on that bullshit.

Especially when they throw the quote at you "blood is thicker than water". First of all the actual quote is "the blood of the covenant is thicker than the water of the womb". So actually saying the family you create is stronger than the one you're born with. Not surprising since they will use anything to get what they want.

You can cut out anyone you want from your life. Partially because you will have to get other people in line with it too. Other people will have to understand that you made the decision and how serious you are about it. That you do not want anyone sharing any info with the person. That sometimes you will not show up to events if the No Contact will be there.

Too many will not agree with what you are doing. They won't see the harm with having them on social and sharing some of what you do on there. Or trying to facilitate some kind of reconciliation. Mostly because they heard a waterdown version of what happened to an outright lie. Which the abuser is good at. And they have rose colored-glasses and believe too much in the Hallmark happy endings.

Toxic and abusive people want to keep the control they had. These people do not like that you are changing. And setting up boundaries to keep yourself happy and healthy ruins that for them. Don't let anyone pull you back, no matter how misguided and well-meaning.

Now, I'm not trying to scare you will all of this. I just want to make you see how far it can go. It can always be about smaller things. Things that are not helpful or just a little mean. You may love the person completely but may only hang out in specific situations. I had one friend that I could never be alone with. They would slowly start to pick at things about me. And they honestly thought they were being helpful in pointing them out. But when we were with other people she did not have as much time to get to that point. There would be too many people and so much going on.

Re-evaluating

And at some point, you will need to re-evaluate if your boundaries are still serving you. Usually, it's not a point that you get rid of one, but more change how you enforce it or loosen some of the parameters. Mostly because you have grown yourself and the people you've allowed around you makes it you so don't really need to them so strong.

You may have also grown so much that it is an automatic response to not be disrespected on certain points. Whatever way works for you. I got to the point of telling people quick that just because I work from home, and sometimes can rearrange my schedule, does not mean I am free to do whatever you want at a drop of a hat. I plan my weeks out and know where it would be easy to move things, and I may just not want to move things around for my own energy. But if you ask nicely and in advance I can help when I can. Try to tell me and you will get nowhere.

If your normal reactions are to protect and respect yourself then the boundary either needs to be lessened or go away. You may need to see what other areas in your life that needs some protection and build up a boundary for that.

Chapter 6

How To Built Your Life To Your Needs

We get a lot of crap for just being who we are. Mostly because it doesn't fit into others' ideas of what is acceptable. That us being "different" makes their lives hard for having to accommodate our unreasonable requests. Even when we don't even ask for things. But who really wants to be all the same?

We all have different life paths and should be able to explore them. Just as not everyone needs to or should go to college, it should not be a necessity to have a better life, people deciding how they want to live their lives.

Changing Your Work

We've all had to change jobs. Quitting to go back to school. Transferring because you are moving away. Or the one everyone understands, finding something that makes you less miserable and pays better. Yet the idea of changing your work just to make yourself happy seems so selfish.

And we get it from everywhere. There is still such a prevalent belief that everyone is miserable at their jobs. So why should you have it any differently? It's such an unhealthy belief that if you're miserable then everyone else should be too. Instead of working to find a better option, or even see if where you are can make some changes. We all want better for our lives and should hold everyone and everything around us to that expectation.

Ok, I'll get off my soapbox.

Anyways, you can make changes that are accommodating to your personality and energy. It's really not you being difficult. The things we want as introverts does not mean we are forcing everyone else to cater to your every need. You're honestly making yourself more productive and a better worker.

When You Don't Quite Want To Leave

There may only be a few things you want to just make things a little easier. You may like what you do, like some of your coworkers, and get paid decently. So the idea now of leaving just isn't really appealing.

Open office plans are the bane of our existence. You can hear what everyone is doing, every freaking click of a keyboard. And others just can't understand how draining (and annoying) that type of environment can be. But there are ways you can combat it.

If your office has empty conference rooms or small offices ask if you can use one for a few hours every week. You can always tell management that you keep getting interrupted and you don't want your work to suffer. Asking for these short periods of time is more understanding and doesn't make you seem like you hate your coworkers. Which is a strangely normal assumption to most when you ask for more privacy at work. People thinking you're not a "team player" can really hurt your relationships there.

If you have client or office meeting calls that do not require you to have a computer ask to have a walking meeting. Even though you are still stuck talking it gets you away from all the extra noise. Bring a small notebook and pen with you if you need to jot down some notes. Of course, this doesn't work if there's a presentation or you need to give a lot of numbers and stats. I wouldn't want to bring all the company information outside.

Set up the expectation that you are not available at certain times. Maybe you have client work that almost always comes in around 10am. So you let people know you want to work on that until lunchtime. So no one should interrupt you unless it's absolutely necessary. Put on some headphones to help signal that. Setting up clear boundaries will help.

Of course, this can be easier said than done. You need to know who at your work can actually make these decisions and who will actually listen to you. You might bring some of these up with other coworkers who're not doing as well in the environment as you. More people can be taken more seriously and less of a "problem".

The bigger option, which now companies can see as a viable option, is to work from home. This may be just a couple of days a week. Companies have seen now that a lot of people can still get their work done and do it securely.

Now, I'm not saying you need to go full-time from home. Even as an introvert you may not do so well working completely alone. Maybe ask for a couple of days. Maybe the busy days of teamwork and meeting are Mondays and Wednesdays so ask for Tuesdays and Thursdays. Or you know Wednesdays are when you have the least amount of energy. There's always a way to work around things.

Time To Move On

You can't get what you need from the job you have you can make sure to include your wants and needs into your next one. Long gone are the times where you stay at one job for decades until you retire. Not because people are not loyal but because companies don't take care of their employees. Some can't or won't give good raises or have ways for people to move up in the company.

And you have every right to go somewhere else that will give you what you need. Not only in a pay raise, but a better environment and culture. I quit a job that had a horrible culture. Different departments hated helping each other and the company would do anything not to pay you for anything.I was done after they tried to force me to clean a self-checkout machine that someone humped and left some liquid on.

When looking for new work you need to know what things you want from it. Do you want the option to work from home a couple of days a week? Do you want an actual office for some privacy? Does the place have dozens of meetings a week, most that could have just been an email?

Working On Your Own

Maybe you want more independence. A little more say in what you do. Especially the idea of exclusively working from home is tempting to a lot of us. Plus we get to make our own schedule, meaning working the times that are most productive for us. On top of that, I can run all my errands when it's not busy.

Of course, when it comes to working on your own, that doesn't always mean you don't have other people calling the shots or don't have to interact with others. And you may not want total isolation. I still like talking to people sometimes. I don't think the whole world is annoying.

But you can build to a business, side hustle, or multiple to make a full-time living and live how you want. I'm not going to go too much into building a business or side hustle here (check out my other book *Living Off The Hustle* for more).

What you do need to figure out what you want to do, the time you want to do it, and how much you want to work with people. These are the first questions I always ask people when they first start figuring things out. The criteria is different between a photographer and life coach, or gardener and graphic designer.

When figuring out what you will there are some really good questions to think over:

- Product or service?
- Do you want regular hours? Less hours? Able to split them up?
- How fast can you finish? How much time do you actually want to do it?

- How much people interaction do you want? Can you handle some big groups? Good with individuals and couples? No kind of customer service at all?
- How much say do you need in what you create? How much does it bother you to have others dictate what you do?

This is just a starting point to help you get started. There's a lot more you will need to figure out before you get started. But you can start small and quick to see how you like it. Not just if it makes money, but how it fits into your life.

Home Life

You can start shaping your own home to make yourself more comfortable. Now, this may sound weird to some because you'd assume that people do that anyways. But you'd be surprised how we (especially as introverts) are being selfish, difficult, and sometimes cruel for wanting things in our lives and home a certain way.

Especially as kids with adults who either didn't care or didn't understand. Like asking to not have the TV too loud when you were trying to study. Or when they had friends over they forced you to let their kids play in your room. Being punished for doing something that they deemed was loud, but ridiculed you for reading.

So as an adult, your home doesn't quite work for you. It honestly took me watching HGTV for a while to figure out why some of the renovations bothered me. So much of what people built was to accommodate other people in their homes. They would have a huge gourmet kitchen even though they hardly cook. But had to have it because one of the mothers love to cook and the extended family loved to hang around the kitchen.

If I ever build a house I will do none of that. No big soaker tube because I don't like baths. Also won't be necessary because I won't be having kids. I will have a huge office since I work from home and actually enjoy what I do. Hell, a library. Even if the house was miraculously several thousand square feet I wouldn't have many guest rooms. I want nobody to stay with me.

You can also create your space for what you want. Now, I know you could be living with other people so not have a say in some areas. Work with what you got. Have a lock on your door for privacy. Put up some cheap canvas (art) on the walls. Canvas is a cloth and will help deaden sound from either direction.

If you have kids, try to have a space that is more for quiet time. For sitting and reading or doing homework. Or have a separate room for the kids. That way most of their noise and mess stays there. I do understand that these are easier said than done and will take time (when they are older) for some of these to stick. Or when you can move to a bigger place.

The Company Your Keep

I can't not throw in here that building a life to your wants and needs also includes the people in it. I've already gone over a lot in the last chapter with boundaries, but I wanted to go over some more specifics and examples. Boundaries are important but I pushed it more for people who don't give too much to your life or you feel like you can't kick out of your life.

But it also counts for the people who have to have in your life with work or people you like but only for so long. There is nothing wrong with not being too friendly with certain co-workers. Or only doing fun things with a specific friend. Like, you wouldn't sit around and have deep discussions but will hit an opening together. Not all relationships in your life need to advance in any way.

And it's to say that these people are bad in any way. You can just have a few things in common or are at different periods in your lives. I have some friends I don't really talk about my business with because it just goes right over their heads. Or that co-worker that you enjoy going out to lunch with during the week, but you don't do anything in the evenings or weekends with them. They may want to stay longer or drink more. What they enjoy may just no be your scene.

The thing to remember for all of this is that people will do this with you. No one should take it personally. We all only have so much time and when you want or have to do certain things some people just don't work.

Hell, one of my closest friends didn't do as much with me when she just had a baby. Mostly because she knew I don't really like them. Not that I wouldn't help if she really needed it, but she wanted to do more with her baby and she knew I would just be really awkward. Now that she is older I'm good with hanging with the kid. I take her to the museum, have fun doing crafts, and even have gone to her karate classes. I get to be the fun, kind of weird aunt.

But you will also want a few more extroverted friends. Just to push you out of your comfort zone sometimes.

And of course, the more laid-back ones for just browsing through a bookstore and sitting at home watching a movie. Fill your life with the people who will enhance your life and not ad stress.

Chapter 7

We Could All Use A Friend

I don't know about you but we are lucky we're forced to be in school most of our childhood. I don't know how I'd have made any friends otherwise. We can be slow to open up sometimes. So being around the same kids week after week can force some bonds. Others can see who you are once you are comfortable. Whether you have the same humor, love the same band, or have a dislike for the same lunch food.

As you get older you start to lose friends. Which isn't a bad thing. People leave for college, move away, and just generally grow apart. But making new friends, as adults, is hard. We do not have those built-in systems that get a lot of people close together.

Working at different places doesn't always offer a good alternative. People come and go at different times. You can have a lot less free time to converse. And just the general work culture and dynamic may not make it easy.

Finding New Friends

At some point in life, you will nee dot make another friend. Whether its because so many have left on their own or you cut them off. In the process of growing and growing up, we have different wants, needs, and interests. So it would be nice to have some people who enjoyed some of those new interests too.

But not being social creatures, that's hard. The good news is we don't need to find many. We do great with a small group of friends anyways. Though we still need to be picky, just a little less worry about compatibility like you would someone you date.

Mining Your Friend Group(s)

This is honestly the first place you should look, the one I overlooked for a long time. I was so used to compartmentalizing different friends into different groups. Where so many never interacted. But if you actually like your friend and trust them to a certain extent, then they might have others friends that you would get along with.

One way to do this is to ask your friend to invite you to some of the gatherings. Gasp, I know. Actually volunteering to go to group gatherings. The horror. But this will be the easy way to see who you could vibe with. No added pressure.

Though the challenge can be the group itself. I've seen it many times where a group will only be tolerant of an outsider and only stick with the core group. Or some of them are perfectly happy with how things are in the group. Not wanting to do anything outside it, including hanging with a new friend.

Even if you don't find anyone with their friends they can help you get out of your bubble a bit. Maybe going to something that they enjoy that you've been curious about.

I'm iffy about saying to try and be friends with a partner's friends. Romantic relations don't always mesh with the group. Plus if anything goes wrong in the relationship the friends will feel a sense of loyalty and pick a side. Which sucks if you broke up amicably or they did something wrong (and people knew about it) they feel like it's against some rule to stay friends. But it doesn't mean you shouldn't try, but I like to give that warning.

Use Your Kids Or Pets

Seriously, use whatever you got. You're not pimping them out. Hell, you're going out more which can always be good for them. Both groups need to have supervision so try to find ones that you can connect to.

It's always a little easier to make friends with other moms when you do mom shit, all the time with your kids. You're all sitting on the side of dance practice or a soccer game. Being miserable at another concert. (I'm not saying you don't love what your kid does but there's always someone performing something cringe-worthy. Especially the younger they are.) sometimes shared misery can bring people together.

Kids and pets can have playdates and go to the park. It will take a while but sooner or later you can find someone you vibe with. Though there will always be the weird ones, the negligent ones, and those who are way too involved. Don't go in there desperate, it just attracts all the crazies. Don't go in with a checklist of what you are looking for. Just be open to finding new people.

And the thing is, these all don't have to be really close friends you're making. They can just be the person you meet up with even Tuesday at the dog park. Or the one you go get coffee with sometimes while waiting for your kids to get out of practice.

Find A Community For Your Interests and Hobbies

It's always good to start off with common interests when getting to know people. So going to meet-ups and events based around a common interest is a good place to start. Of course, it's easier the closer you are to the city to find a variety. But there are always online groups to connect with.

It is literally something out there for everyone. There is a group out there for people who keep killing all their plants but are desperate to keep something alive. Groups for you OTP (One True Pairing) for that one character in that book that only shows up for a chapter. (Or even your NOTP, which is just your despise of a pairing.)

For the most part, you can just be a casual participant and still find people to talk to. Of course with most things online there are the assholes and gatekeepers who just try to make things difficult. But there are plenty out there that will just want to talk. Even better then they have no problems with questions.

I've met some great women in some of the meet-ups I've gone to. The two I still go to are Tuesdays Together and Women In Podcasting. We've gone to art fairs, conferences, and met up for lunch. Another great place to mine is Facebook groups. You can search by interest and location. That's how I found those two because I wanted something in person.

Don't Be Something You're Not

This goes without saying but I know it can be hard not to fall into this. But being yourself when meeting new people (even when dating) will make it more likely you will find people that you will enjoy.

Yeah, we always want to show our best selves at first. Also not drop everything on people. One, it's not fair to anyone and a little unhealthy. Two, you don't even know if you can trust people with that info. Most people will find out that I love dogs early on. It's a good way to see if we have that in common but also if they are the kinds of people who hate dogs that don't think they deserve any kindness. Good luck without a soul, we can't be friends. But it will be a little while before people realize how *obsessed* I am with them. Like I memorize as many breeds as I can. I will stop in the middle of a conversation to point out a dog. Even walk away from if said dog looks like it wants me to pet it.

All the people close to me know this and accept it. We all know I'm weird. If you want to be friends with me that is just the reality. So don't constantly force yourself to go out to parties, always go out to noisy places, or only do what the other person wants to do. You should be getting to know both of your likes. Yes, open yourself to new experiences and be accommodating sometimes.

There are some people you may not be great, close friends with and you only do certain things together. That is perfectly fine. In college, I had a friend that we only went out dancing together. But since it was only a couple of times a month it didn't make me feel bad about being up. It also worked because she wasn't a heavy drinker (and I don't drink) and we both really just wanted to dance and not talk to people.

Nurturing The Ones You Have

People do not realize that once you get out of school it's hard to keep your friends, not just make new ones. We all grow up and go different ways. And there's nothing wrong with that. But as time goes on you still need to adjust some so the friends you do keep stay. You should be able to share things about yourselves and find new things about yourselves.

Show Your Appreciation

The idea is that you guys can do things for each other. No matter the level o your friendship there should be some give and take. Buying each other coffee. Spotting one for gas. Or course this isn't about always expecting something in return, but some trust that you will help each other every once in a while.

Give and Allow Yourself To Trust

We are hard to get to know right away. We are slow to open up, partially because that's just part of our personality and partially because we have had too much experience of people having problems with parts of us. Especially when we are in school. Even the smallest crack can be used against us real quick when it's given to the wrong person.

So we have to allow ourselves to trust people. That we can trust ourselves to pick people who will accept us. Who will use parts of us against us. And I know some people will not like me saying this, but you do not have to completely trust everyone. Most people should not get your complete trust.

It depends on what kind of friendship you have which depends on how much you tell the other person and how deep you can go. We've all had friends where we just had one thing in common. You can still have fun, go out for that one thing and still hang, but your conversations never get real deep. They are not the person to go to for real problems. Not to say it's a bad relationship, that's just what you established it to be. That's how far you trust them.

You've had co-workers that you know you can talk about things with and others you know will gossip the hell out of your business. Each person will be different and it will be trial and error. Some people will surprise you in what they want the friendship to be and can be there for you for the hard shit.

Allow Vulnerability

Along with trust is allowing yourself to be vulnerable. Of course, this does not mean you let everything out with everyone. Each person gets only so much as you can trust them with. Again, they need to earn seeing the hard parts of you. But that kind of openness allows for more and better connections.

We've all been pushed to be strong and take care of things ourselves. But it is not a weakness to want or need help. To actually ask for things that are out of your control. The thing is too, allowing yourself to be vulnerable may be more working through things with a therapist and then showing parts of what you learned after all the work with people.

These connections don't always have to be about past hurts or fears. It can be finally telling someone you miss them or even 'I love you'. That opening in the hopes that the other person will return the feeling is what allows for that connection. To show that you are worthy. Vulnerability is key to connection because it is the courage to be open to another human. It's allowing yourself to be open to a person to get close to you. Giving without conditions or expectations.

Be Consistent

Even if you don't see each other often you still need to keep in touch in some way, consistently. Of course, what the means will be up to your relationship. Depending on how the friendship is and both of your wants and needs. Plus what both of your Love Languages* are, by way of saying how you express your love.

As I said earlier, mine is Quality Time so having time spent together is what's important. Yes, hanging and having deep discussions are my jam but just being able to sit in the same room enjoying our own things works for me too. One friend we send running memes and videos to each other.

Again, works for me because it shows that she was thinking of me and she gave me a laugh.

The point of friendships is that you are there for each other. Someone to hang with, talk to, and just be yourself. We all get busy and some things can take over for a while. You need to work on keeping it alive. I know for some of us we get used to the extroverted friends being the pushers and callers. That we fall back on that and don't put in as much effort. But a friendship can fade if both sides are putting in close to the same amount of effort and energy.

You Do Need To See People and Talk To Them

I know, shocking. But since these are people you already know and supposedly like you should want to hang with them. Not everything can be done online or through messages. I can be a hermit sometimes with the best of them but I still get out see people.

I always try to get out of the house to see some people a few times a month. Again, this is on both your schedules so you can just have a quick coffee meet-up if that's all the time or energy you have. Some of your friends will want to talk on the phone with you and it would be rude not to some of the time. Whatever the friendship needs. I have one who I've know since Junior High that we mostly communicate with funny videos and memes.

And you will need to do some things that they want to do more than you don't want to. It's suppose to be a give and take. I could care less about baby showers, but I will go to them because I want to support my friend. Plus I can the organized one that's just a little helper. Not like I can chime in about all the stuff about kids. I'm just going to be the fun, kind of weird, aunt.

You Are Worthy

I don't think this is a particular introvert problem, but I wanted to touch on it because it can be an issue. And that's the fear that we are not good enough to be friends with the people in our lives. That we're not doing enough, we're annoying, or that we make things way too difficult. To some people, you will always be too much.

There are people out there that will enjoy, respect, and love you for you. You never have to change who you are to get someone to like you. There should never be hoops you have to jump through to prove yourself to anyone. These people should want the best for you and that should include what they bring into your life. That things that truly make you happy will never be a problem. But they will also be your cheerleader when you want to better yourself.

Making Sure You Both Get What You Need

Now this does not mean that you can tell people "this is how I am, deal with it". That is manipulative and bordering on abusive. Yes, people should accept you for who you are but they don't have to take any of your crap. Or the other way around. No one should be making anyone else's life harder, actively or not.

Friendship means you both get something from the relationship. It can simply be just someone to talk about one shared interest all the way to this is the person you would call to help hide a body. Each person should be giving to the other. Whether s it time, support, and shoulder to cry on, or someone to bail them out of jail. You need to make sure what you need out of any relationship you have then make sure you get it. And the means that you need to be at least asking that you are giving what the other person needs too.

And you may realize that the relationship isn't giving you really anything. The other person can just be a complainer that never does anything to change the circumstances or someone who always tries to steer the conversation back to them. The main point of the chapter was to make and keep friends but sometimes, after talking to the other person, you may not want to keep it anymore.

Again, this goes back to your boundaries. You should not be putting time and energy into a friendship that will not put any back to you. The nice thing about introverts is that we really don't need a big group of friends. Having 2-3 is actually pretty perfect. Even better when one of them is extroverted and they invite you to other things with other people. Just got my quota of people for the next 2 weeks.

Chapter 8

Romance: Dating and Relationships

Most of us want a relationship, to be loved. Hell, we should excel at it since it's just one-on-one talking and all that jazz. But it's never that simple. Once you add other people to the mix things get complicated. But that can be the best part. The extra spice and a safe place to be. The point of all of this is to have a partner that has your back and grows a life together. It's up to you what that life is. Whether or not it means marriage, kids, or the whole shi-bang.

The thing is to know what it is you want to and need so you know what you are looking for. And you won't know all the answers right away. You can realize what you thought you wanted wasn't right. Or you could change your mind later because of a life change or your just in another stage in your life. You don't even need to be looking for forever right now.

Flirting

I have no problem saying I suck at this. To say that I am oblivious to others trying to get my attention is an understatement. I've only dated one person, who became my future ex-husband, and it took a village to get us dating. To say that I really needed to research for this part, mostly for myself, was not an understatement. Cause I need *help*.

The Five Flirting Styles by Dr. Jeffrey Hall* has the best descriptions. I found them to be pretty good ideas in a deferred general idea, but everything can fall into one or the other and be very helpful.

- **Playful** and this is just basically flirting for fun without having any expectations. It is more of lighthearted flirting.
- **Physical** where you flirt using your body language e.g by touching a person. I could say by actual physical contact or how your body is turned towards the person.
- **Polite.** This entails having more proper manners and maintaining non-sexual communication. That means being polite and asking certain questions that make the other person feel like you genuinely want to know about them.
- **Sincere:** This is where you're genuinely interested in what they are talking about because you want to develop an emotional connection. Here you are more engaged with what they do and you're trying to figure out some things that you connect with; things that are similar for both of you guys. You also listen to note your different opinions and stuff like that.

· **Traditional.** This is just following the same (old school) courtship rules of 'Who asked who out first', 'Who pays for things', etc. For example, I really like the idea of someone getting the door for me.

However, we all appreciate that, as introverts, we cannot be comfortable taking part in some of the described ways of flirting, especially if in clubs or bars or generally loud public spaces. We are more inclined towards more meaningful meetings and relationships, not the casual engagements that most of the above flirting styles lean towards. Dr. Hall says most introverts relate to the 'Sincere' or 'Polite' styles. I know I can't be the center of attention at a party, I barely go to parties! I can't be loud or boisterous. I definitely am not touchy-feely. But I also know that I like asking people questions. I love hearing stories from people. I love feeling that they are interested in me as well. We exchange stories. We see that we have connections with different ideas in our family and our beliefs.

It's Not A Numbers Game

This is honestly the worst thing to say if you're trying to encourage an introvert to date. Numbers mean multiples, meaning going on many many first dates. That sounds horrifying and exhausting to go through so many first dates with all the 'getting to know you' questions and worrying that we're being weird.

Yes, you will have to go on more than one. But that doesn't mean you literally need to see a new person every other day just because statistically there's a better chance of finding a great person. We all should be a little bit discerning. Not just at anyone that wants to have a date. That looks more like an easy way to find a manipulator, abuser, or even a serial killer. We all have preferences, so use them.

That doesn't make you picky. Or that you are not giving enough people a chance. You have every right to choose who gets any kind of access to you. No one should get a pass through your boundaries just because you're looking for love.

And most of us are not running around with wildly superficial requirements. I would never date a smoker. I think it's absolutely disgusting and I'm allergic. Same with someone who has to like animals. Now they don't have to be as enthusiastic as me, cause I even know I can be a bit much. No one should ever start from a place of tolerating things you don't like.

While on the other side a guy might just need me to tolerate his love of sports. I honestly could not care about it, but it doesn't bother me if he went to games or watched it every Sunday. Even to the point of him whooping as a good play or something. Now if he was loud or wanted to watch with a bunch of friends then something would have to be worked out. If I'm at home I don't want that shit around. They can go to a bar or someone else's or plan enough ahead so I can be somewhere else. Just don't expect me to cook for it or have to watch and be excited too.

What you do and do not want in a relationship is just as valid. We would never work if you needed me to really love your cat. Not saying I wouldn't want to, but I'm allergic. Just as I would want someone who would more than tolerate dogs. Whatever works for your lifestyle.

Just as a side note, I want everyone to get out of their head the idea that you should be with someone just because you love them. Love is never enough. Not sorry to burst your bubble.

Not only should there be some commonality between you to but also respect, trust, honesty, and commitment. Someone who keeps trying to force you to go partying every weekend because they think you'll have more fun that way doesn't really respect who you are. Or someone who won't discuss finances with you does not trust you.

Dating

We all get lonely sometimes. We all want to have some companionship in life. Someone to hang with, have inner jokes, and know you have each others' back. Now, this does sound exactly like a friend and it is. You should be with people you can be friends with. That is the point of being together. There is just some added attraction to it. But I always want to remind people that your standards for friends should be the same for dating. You should not have to change or hide yourself to have their attention.

Now I'm not gonna lie, I'm not very good at this. And since I've been out of the game for an extended time it's a whole new landscape for me. But it's just as hard as finding new friends. So much is online now and a lot can get lost in communication.

Online

This is a whole new beast from when I firsts looked into it in the beginning. There are so many options depending on common interests, age, ethnicity, and even fetishes. Even the sites for "regular" dating each have their quirks and demographics. But it's still a good place to state. Over 50% of hetero and homosexual people find people online*. And the beginning steps can be done in the comfort of your own home

But it can still feel anxiety-ridden because there's so much out there. Even if you're not wading through a crowd of people and trying to talk about all the noise. Some just have a profile you fill out while others have personality tests that plays into the matches. Of course, if you go for the paid option you have more of a chance of finding someone who is looking for something serious than just a hookup. Some are pretty good at matching people with similar interests and energies. But there's also the worry about how much to put on the profiles. What's safe in general and what's just TMI.

We can be great starting out because we can be more expressive in writing. But some of the nuances can be lost to us. On the other end, it's hard because there are so many options out there. Even if you only wait for others' to contact you first. You can only connect too far through a screen. I'm decent with video calling but I'd rather skip it. And at some point, you still have to meet in person.

Take Your Hobbies Into The World

I've already covered this some in the last chapter. Always having something you enjoy that is fun is a good way to show someone the best parts of you. And if you are somewhere that's set up just for the hobby that sets you up to know the other person likes it enough to go too. For a lot of our hobbies, we do them alone or with the same few people

There are a lot of events and services out there that set up dates and group settings can be a good idea. The part I caution about is doing something way out of your comfort zone. Yeah, a lot of people there may not be good at the thing too but it can be too distracting. Some of us can be very embarrassed if we mess up. It can be too new that we don't open up as much. Or we get so consumed with learning and trying to get it right that we don't really talk to the other people, miss queues, and may just spend the time enjoying the activities alone (oh shit, that may be me).

When You're With An Extrovert

It happens to the best of us. When you hit it off with someone you can't really stop the feelings. And nothing says being with an extrovert can't work. It's honestly one of the least of your problems.

The main thing is to set up early on what energy levels you both have, and what needs you both have. Don't try to change or match each other if it isn't what's natural to you. That's giving them a false idea of who you are. And you should be able to be honest and accepted for who you are.

Once you know what each others' needs are for energy and stimulation you need to figure what parts you can actually be a part of. A lot of people get this part wrong. You should not be the only person who meets all their needs. That's what their friends and family are for. The same people they already did some of these things with. That shouldn't stop. Just sometimes you're added in.

On the other side, you want them to go out without you sometimes. This is how you get some alone time. Time to sit and read or play a game with no interruptions. You two don't stop being individuals with some different interests. Not everything should be shared and done together. Keep up your other relationships, including the one with yourself.

One Of You Will Be More Outgoing Than The Other

If you find yourself dating an introvert don't think it'll be smooth sailing. We are human and complicated people and nothing can ever be simple. The one thing I've noticed when I find two people who are together and both introverts is that neither are the same level. When you think about it in general you think "of course that's logical". Yet when the relationship moves along that goes right out the door.

They always think it's great; no one to pressure you to go out more, good with being home alone more, or no loud noises. And it is good because you can understand that part of each other more. But we are all different and the introvert/extrovert is a sliding scale, not an either-or.

There will be things that you find ok to do that your other doesn't enjoy at all. One will want to stay in more days than the other. And you both go through cycles, rarely syncing up. Just like everything else in a relationship your individual wants and needs will all play a part. For me, I don't really enjoy big parties and loud gatherings, but getting together with my large extended family is great fun for me. My ex didn't always do well with that dynamic because he didn't like "being filtered". Pretty much being a little better behaved in front of my grandparents so as not to be rude while he really enjoyed talking about anything and everything and getting drunk.

Not saying one was better than the other, just it was a clashing of what we enjoyed. While one could enjoy being alone to relax but have different needs for noise. I prefer to have things more on the quiet side. I like music to fill a room but I don't need the volume so high that I can hear everything on a different floor through a closed door. Some are fine with that with certain things, like watching a movie or playing games. Others really need things quiet.

How To Be A Better Partner

After some time, you get comfortable, maybe get to the point of marriage. One of the problems is that too many get too comfortable. We all do a little less of the spontaneous things. We stop doing the little things to show we're thinking of the other or that we even care. Not appreciating what the other does for us. Everyone already hears about still having date nights, even when you have kids, but isn't enough.

Even though we introverts are all about deep talks we can stop doing it with our partners. Just being used to them and think we've heard it all. But as time goes on we all grow and things in life change. Sometimes our priorities shift and we need to be open about them. Still listen to each other. About the small things to still talking about your futures. Still keep each other up to date on things happening. You are supposed to be a team so let the other know if you're going to be late at work or plan to hang with friends.

Keep up with your self-care. Sometimes we can get engulfed and so focused on our relationship that we keep putting ourselves on the side. To be a better partner (worker, parent, etc) we need to take care of ourselves. Do some of the things we love by ourselves. Not everything you do needs to be together, even if you both are in the same house. Part of the connection is that you are both comfortable enough to just do your own thing. And don't let anyone make you feel bad for doing your own thing. It's healthy and no one needs to be in your business all the time.

Trust and respect goes both ways. Sometimes you need to remind a partner how you want to be treated. We all can get too comfortable and possibly lazy, life happens. But you do not need it to keep going. And they have every right to remind you of this too. We choose the people we are with and you can change your mind if you are not getting your needs met.

Chapter 9

Being A Parent

Not gonna lie, I'm not a parent. But that doesn't mean I can't give some advice about introverted kids. One, I still remember a lot from when I was a kid and don't try to forget about it now that I'm an "adult". Two, I've talked to several specialists and a bunch of actual parents. So they steered me when I might have been wrong or had no idea.

You need to accept that your introverted child will not be a social butterfly. There is nothing wrong with them or that they need therapy to be more extroverted and "acceptable". Not pushing these points can actually help them grow up to be well-rounded adults. I was lucky that my parents were not pushy about things. We got to explore ourselves more. Yeah, it may have taken a little longer to find our paths but we got there unscathed. Plus we didn't need to act out just to be heard.

Not gonna lie, I'm not a parent. But that doesn't mean I can't give some advice about introverted kids. One, I still remember a lot from when I was a kid and don't try to forget about it now that I'm an "adult". Two, I've talked to several specialists and a bunch of actual parents. So they steered me when I might have been wrong or had no idea.

Having Very Mixed Personality Kids

It's hard enough to give kids what they need. Making sure they're not on a screen too long, eating enough veggies, or getting them to do their homework so they won't live in your basement well into their 30s. But you also have to help with their social and mental needs.

I know you know that your kids are individuals, with their different quirks and personalities. So each kid should be handled differently. When you have more than one it's pretty normal for them to be at least somewhat different. If you are lucky they will get along and can play and hang. Me and my brother are both introverts but the activities we did were only the same half the time. We both played games and would play together a lot of time. But he did not read like I inhaled them. He never cared about doing school sports while I did half of high school. He would rather have his friends come over to hang out and I'd rather go to their houses.

Just like anything with children you are going to have to work on how you interact with them and how they are in the world. You still need to give them your time and attention. Do not spend more on the kid you think is "easier". Whether that's the one more like you and the one who needs more actions from you (like dropping them off somewhere). You are the adult, you need to figure it out.

When You're Introverted But Your Kids Are Not

Oh boy, this seems like its own kind of hell. Not in a horrible way because you have to take care of your kids. You want to do the best for them. But that means them having friends over all the time, planning parties, and driving them to events and sports things. Cause these days you are supposed to be really involved in these things, especially when they are younger.

Now if you're lucky the other parent can take some of this load too. Or your kid can have other parents help out and only need you for some of the stuff. But only if they make decent friends. Not to say in high school I didn't do a lot of stuff. But before I got my license I pretty much did a lot of things on my own. That was just me. But other than that me and my brother pretty much stayed home or just hung with friends.

But you are going to have to be open to do what your kids need. Concerts, recitals, games, and any other thing (that is actually good for them) that they need from you. So you are going to need to plan out your recharging time a lot more stringently. You guard that time just as strongly as you do your children. Because if you are exhausted you are not giving all that they need. And that makes no one happy.

These are the times you lean on your community. Whatever you can get help with from the other parent, family, friends, and even their friends' parents. You need to accept that your child may not like doing all the things you like to do. They may enjoy being around people a lot more and you will let them. Just because we all agree that standing around with other parents you barely know making small talk and having a meeting about fundraising sounds horrible doesn't mean you can skip it.

Having Introverted Kids When You're Not

Sadly this is where many parents can go wrong. Not purposefully or maliciously. But a lot of conventional wisdom out there is still outdated. Not even in reference to being an introvert. Some still believe in heavy gender dividing. Boys not being allowed to cry, girls told to always follow other's lead. That some actually prefer it if the girl was quieter and follows what people tell her (?).

Now, this part is not really meant for you, but more if the other parent or other important people in your child's life. They can be doing things that can be detrimental to the child without even knowing it. This will be the point where you will have to step in, not accusatory but you need to make sure to do what's best for the child.

Especially when kids are young there is so much pressure for them to react accelerated benchmarks. Parents get scared that they are not developing enough to set them up for a good future. But us not making friends fast enough or talking as much as everyone else does not mean we are stunted and even handicapped. I didn't talk as much around one teacher and she got me set up with a speech impediment expert with the school. Not even thinking that I didn't talk because she always made a point to correct what I was saying and that I had a slight accent because my dad did. They actually treated me and my brother like there was something wrong with us because we had an accent.

Gotta love small towns.

Things To Look Out For

Being a parent is never easy. Each child will have their own personality and problems. They are growing humans that have no idea what is going on; in the world or with their bodies. And with a society that pushes for more extrovert traits. But there are some general things I know almost every introverted child will have to go through. It sucked for me and I would rather you help a kid not have to go through any of these alone.

Pushing Us Out Of Our Comfort Zone Can Cross Over To Something Not Good A Lot Sooner Than You Think

Yes, we all need to learn and try new things. But it actually hurts us if we do it constantly. Never having time to do things we find enjoyable and calming gives us a lot of stress. Any especially with the idea that some home we are 'stunted', 'not trying enough', or don't know what's good for us. The point of growing up figuring this out. And even at a young age, we can figure out our own wants and needs.

Yes, we all need to learn and try new things. But it actually hurts us if we do it constantly. Never having time to do things we find enjoyable and calming gives us a lot of stress. Any especially with the idea that some home we are 'stunted', 'not trying enough', or don't know what's good for us. The point of growing up figuring this out. And even at a young age, we can figure out our own wants and needs.

You should be trying to push them, in some things. Kids do not need to be "developing" all the time. They do not need to be in an activity every chance they can. All kids need time to be alone or not have everything so structured. Always going to playdates and not realizing that your kid is not having a good time. Possibly because they have been going from one thing to another and just have no more energy. Or the group you are forcing them to place with never lets them decide what they are doing. Just because it's convenient for you doesn't mean it's good for your kid.

Each kid will have things they are better at than others. It breaks my heart to see some children spending half of their time after school with tutors. Even if they are not bad at a subject. They are just not straight-A students. Even as young as first grade. Your kid having perfect scores is not necessary at all. There are doctors, engineers, scientists, and pilots who were not great at school. And for most of those just being average just to get into college is enough. It's getting into Grad school and enter a Ph.D. program that you need to do a bit better.

None of my grades in high school was ever looked at after I got into college. And nothing in my record in college was ever seen after I got my Bachelor's. No one cares about that shit. Being average in a lot of things is not the end of the world. Some of the best writers out there hardly talk to people. Not all of us are going to talk on stages need to network for work. Not all lawyers go into courtrooms.

Each kid will have things they are better at than others. It breaks my heart to see some children spending half of their time after school with tutors. Even if they are not bad at a subject. They are just not straight-A students. Even as young as first grade. Your kid having perfect scores is not necessary at all. There are doctors, engineers, scientists, and pilots who were not great at school. And for most of those just being average just to get into college is enough.

It's getting into Grad school and enter a Ph.D. program that you need to do a bit better.

None of my grades in high school was ever looked at after I got into college. And nothing in my record in college was ever seen after I got my Bachelor's. No one cares about that shit. Being average in a lot of things is not the end of the world. Some of the best writers out there hardly talk to people. Not all of us are going to talk on stages need to network for work. Not all lawyers go into courtrooms.

Us Blowing Up Is The Last Straw and A Lot Of Built-up

Yes, it can seem rude and disrespectful but when we get to a point of blowing up at someone it is kind of your fault. Because we have been forced to interact, do things for everyone else, and make life easier for others and got get what we need. You are the adult. Your child does not know how to figure out their emotions. They don't know what they are tired and angry about. They learn by example on how to regulate their emotions. That is your job.

You should be the one who can see when they are done and have no energy. You should care that they are getting their needs met, even if it offends someone else because they do not (or won't) understand. It takes us a while to get to that breaking point where we can't hold it in anymore. Where we tried to ask for it and it got pushed aside.

We don't want it to get to this point. We know it makes us look bad and our needs get ignored because others feel justified in being insulted by our reaction that nothing changes. Listen to your kids and advocate for them. For a good chunk of my childhood, my parents were divorced and one did not understand this at all. So after a while, I had to take care of myself with this. Sometimes I had to get mean. But it was the only way anyone would stop bothering me, touching me, or try to force me to do things I didn't want to do.

And don't get all huffy that I should "respect" people. I was respectful up to a point then they lost it and its goes both ways. I never did this for actual reasonable things like schoolwork or following rules. I should not have had to figure things out on my own. My own emotions, my boundaries, or protecting myself.

Believe Us When We Say Something

I never got it when people always thought that children lie. And in the same breathe say that you want them to come to you whenever they had a problem. You pretty much contradicted yourself and even when young a kid will start to understand that. Yeah, I know they can make up stories but isn't usually about seeing a dog that was '10 feet tall' and other exaggerations like that. In the process of raising them, I'm assuming you are teaching them right from wrong and what is bad manners. It may take a while for them to grasp it completely, but it's been talked about.

So when an introvert (or any child) comes up to you to tell you something and they are worried or uncomfortable, you should listen. We do not want to be trouble or upset anyone. It's enough anxiety to talk to an adult as it is especially the older you get because you start to learn that some of them don't react well.

Because if you don't believe us the first time or brush it off as being sensitive then we may never bring it up to you again. And we know now that you are not someone we can trust with these types of things. Which is bad to downright dangerous. Even if it is a small thing in the whole grand scheme of life, a child does not know that. A lot of these things they are seeing and feeling for the first time. They have no knowledge or experience with anything.

Each little thing you don't listen to or brush off will just build-up to show that you don't listen. Which will roll right into us realizing we don't have to listen to you. And that will make the teenage years worse than they ever had to be.

Chapter 10

School Life

We all have to go to school. For some it's a good experience, others not so much. But since it's such a huge part of our young lives it needs to be addressed. Even though I am well into my adult years and have been out of any kind of school for a while I still remember a lot of being in school. I've never forgotten what it is to be the new kid. Being scared about not making any friends. Being able to keep up with my classes.

Just because I'm an "adult" now doesn't mean I can't empathize. And you, as a parent, should not either. They will have many of the same fears, just different circumstances. And we need to remember to actually listen to them to what their problems are.

Do not be like the older generation that just told us to suck it up because we didn't "know" what hard was. We were just spoiled kids who had it easy and want everything handed to us. Which is a load of hypocritical crap. Don't do that to your kids. Listen and watch them because sometimes they won't feel like they can talk to you about things, but if you pay attention you can see that some-things wrong.

We know better what things they are going through. The growing pains and hormonal imbalance. We, as adults, should be guiding them through it so they don't have to suffer alone. To give them context and lessons so they can figure things out on their own.

And there are some particular things you have to look out for your introverted child (or yourself if you're younger). Because we can start off quiet and reserved. It can make us seem a little unfriendly or an easy target.

Being The New Kid

It sucks anytime you have to leave so much of what you know and start over. Getting used to a new place, know-ing where things are in the area, and making new friends. Not trying to age myself, but most of my school years did not have social media so keeping in touch with old friends was never easy. For a lot of kids, especially younger, it's out sight out of mind. And you have to find your new place wherever you are.

And each school and neighborhood has its own dynam-ics that you have to figure out. Who are the bullies, the nosy ones, or what would get people looking at you weird with-out you even knowing? There will already be preconceived ideas around that you will already fall into. By who's in your family, the size of it, where you live in relation to the "good" or "bad" areas, and how you fit into the already established norms.

Now not all of these are bad. They can welcome you and believe you will fit in well. Or not. Some may not like the changing of demographics. And as kids, you may not understand all the dynamics going on. You just want to make friends and have fun. As an adult, you need to keep in mind these things will affect your kids. We all know too well how a lot of what children learn and how they act is a direct result of their parents' actions and beliefs.

When it comes to school there's already the added pressure of being new. Not knowing if there are outright bullies, how accepting they are of outsiders, and whether the teachers there are any good. Then as an introvert, we have to talk to all the new people and figure out where we can fit in.

Fitting In

As I've said before, I've done a lot of moving in my life so I got pretty good at fitting in real quick in school just to stave off any trouble. And some of those times I was in another state and country. There are some things that are just true for all schools.

Of course, these are suggestions for being new in school and in the beginning. It's more for safety and is in no way telling people to change who they are.

Don't Go All-in With The First Person Who's Nice To You

This goes in two ways. It can be someone that is not liked at the school and is actually bad but is desperate to make a friend that they will latch onto anyone. Or they are actually bullies and will either play a prank on you or try to get something on you to use against you. Someone had tried to do this at least a third of the time. Some people just want an easy target.

I'm not saying don't be nice or completely ignore them. But pay attention. Does no one else ever talk to you after that? Do you get weird looks? Make sure you try to interact with other people in your classes. Sooner or later someone will say something. Either to warn you because they see that you're nice and should know or they let it slip because they find it funny.

Keep your options open. Just like you, other people will need to take time to open up. Another thing I learned early is that some people do not open their friend group unless forced to so it may be too hard to get in and that can show you that if they are "trying" it's not for good reasons. Now the main core group can be the same friends for a decade, but if they rarely talk to other people in class if one of the core is around then it's suspect.

Start Off Wearing More Neutral Clothes

Again, I'm not saying change who you are and conform. We all have outfits that are just a little toned down. Whether it's just a comfy outfit or something you wear around relatives so they don't pick on you. That doesn't mean you need to wear completely neutral and have no personality. You are already going to stand out for being new. Sadly if your clothes are seen as "showy" or "flashy" some will think that you trying to show off or have everyone look at you. And they will put a target on your back for it.

In high school, I was a bit into punk rock. Not full-blown but I enjoyed some of the clothes and music. But I did not dress it the first week of a new school. I didn't dress preppy or girly because that's not my style but I kept it a t-shirt and jeans. People can be awful and some will try to find something easy to grab at, even adults.

Stay In The Middle Of The Crowd Until You Know The Dynamics

This is expanding on the clothes part. Don't try too hard to make friends right away, but also not repel them. Believe me, it sucks having to temper yourself just so you don't have a shit time at school.

This goes for everything and each school will need to have a different amount of time for you to figure it out. Some things are subtle no can take a few weeks to show themselves. Especially if it's the beginning of the year. Everyone is trying to find the normal to a new grade, teachers, and some friends being moved around. And this isn't just for the students. You need to figure out what teachers will generally allow and not allow, and who are the people who can get away with more things. And it's not always the popular kids getting away with awful shit. Sometimes it's marching band coming and going whenever they want. Or the smart, kind of quiet ones who can get away with things because they are never a problem with the teachers (....may or may not have been me).

Some teachers try to find their "favorites" and that's not always a good thing. These are the people who they always call on because you pay attention more, but will be annoyed when you can't answer the question even though you've been the one who had to answer 40% throughout the whole class. Or the ones they like to make examples of. Or The

Who they want to use for their own personal spy. I've been lucky that most of my teachers were not horrible, but they are all human and I know how weird people can be.

Sometimes We Can Have Trouble In School

Sadly we can be overlooked when we have problems. When things go wrong we usually don't make noise. We don't disrupt, we close in farther into ourselves. To the point it can take a while for anyone to notice anything is wrong.

And too many times we get blamed for those things. As children you don't know what to do, you get overwhelmed and do what's natural. But then some much of the time when people notice it's because our grades are too low or we're threatened with detention for not doing work.

It's Hard To Ask For Help

Asking for help requires talking. Which is hard enough as a kid, to an adult. Having to admit that we don't understand. Plus, a lot of the time in front of the rest of the class. Not exactly the best circumstances. On top of that, if someone else already had a question on the same thing it makes us feel worse. One for feeling stupid after it was explained again. And two for being a bother in some way. Then we get lower grades because we still didn't get what we needed, making us feel even worse.

And some of the times you have a question isn't the "time" when the teacher wants to be interrupted. So you can be seen as a problem, even though you had to muster all your strength to even raise your hand. Not to mention that kids can be awful too. There is always one bully out there that can find the quiet ones and go after them. They will find something to pick on. And because you don't say things it will continue.

Some Classes Rely Heavily On Participation

Participation sucks. Nobody wants to have to raise their hands and answer questions, especially if they do not know the answer. Hell, I was actually good in school and knew the answer most of the time. Still didn't want to answer.

There's always those same couple of people who hog all the time. Or the teacher fires at you too quickly that you don't have time to process. Then you look and feel stupid because you can't answer. Hell, sometimes the teacher makes an example out of you (wrongfully) like you did something wrong. Yeah, that really makes anybody want to participate even more (eye roll).

A few things I've done to participate just enough to get credit have been to ask or answer questions early. Partially so you don't have as much time to worry about when the right time is to get in. Things, in the beginning, are usually easier and quicker. Hell, sometimes I would talk to some of my friends and see what questions they had on the homework and ask it for them. Now, this doesn't always work every time and with every teacher. If the teacher wants everyone to take turns reading or everyone has to do a presentation then you can't get around that. But this can help take the pressure and anxiety off some of your classes.

Group Projects

If you can get the right people group projects can be fun. You're not doing everything yourself and someone else can be more upfront for presenting. But that doesn't always happen. Sometimes you get the lazy ones who won't work at all. Others just want to delegate. Or the ones who try to change who does what so they can just take parts of what you already worked on.

The problem with this is standing up for yourself. Maybe the teacher will keep the trouble makers in check, but the older you get the more you'll have to check them yourself. Sometimes you just work with the system. Like when things are divided you make sure it gets put in writing and then talk to the teacher about it. So they know what you are doing as a witness.

There have been times where I have refused to work with people because it would just be easier to do it myself. I was lucky that my teachers were good with it. I was a good student who didn't cause problems. One teacher has so the people who got the highest scores for a quiz got to work as a group for the test. Some of the time I just did it solo because some of the people would only study for the quiz just so they could get the smart kids to help them with the test. Boy did it piss them off when I'd say I'd take my test alone. I would be done faster and have time to just read while everyone else finished.

Being Perceived As Easy

Just because we can be quiet and get our work done doesn't mean we can't struggle. We're more likely than not to say when there is a problem. We will try to. Figure things out ourselves. And there is the added pressure that everyone puts on you for being 'so easy'. So we keep on not saying anything because it makes people happy. There are always other students who have more trouble figuring things out or who are more disruptive.

Then this gets into a habit with most of the rest of your life. So you don't try to cause problems to parents, friends, or even at work. Which is not good for you. You will not get what you need when things actually go wrong. It can get downright dangerous. This can be when you don't go to the doctor if you don't feel right and some kind of harassment at work. Not gonna need to say how that's bad and enforced for girls....

My very first job I had a scary interaction with a coworker. Since I was only 15 I was only allowed to work with the ice cream stations throughout Camp Snoopy. One morning I'm opening with a guy who was hired a few weeks after me. Nothing wrong with talking about what's going on in life. But he quickly started an whether or not I had a boyfriend. How much "experience" did I have. Then said he could teach me some things if I wanted but we would have to keep quiet about it. I barely responded to any of these things and my mind was racing because I knew no one would be by to check on us for at least an hour. The next station, which was in sight, would have anyone at it for 30 minutes and they would be busy with their setup.

So I had to worry about this guy who was more than twice my size and in his 20s who could trap me in the backroom or freezer. Especially since it was a weekday and it could be hours be we saw anyone near. Some days the leads wouldn't even stop by until close to lunch. And there were a lot of spots behind the counter to get cornered. To say I was relieved when someone showed up an hour after open is an understatement. But I couldn't tell the lead right away and they were not really listening because we got busy.

I had to wait until the next day to get a manager to talk to them about it. It already felt awful because there was already suspicions about why I said this about him. Plus they had a bunch of meetings that day and me talking to them took time out of their schedule. It wasn't until 2 weeks later that I heard anything about any action. And I had to work with him one other time. Then it took a different manager and a couple of leads to question all the females again. Because I was not the first person to say anything and a bunch of others did after me. Some of us were not even reported or told to others.

He had put his hands on at least one of the other girls. I was the one he got the most graphic with but maybe because I was not as nice about my answers or steered real clear of him. But because I already had the habit of not being trouble for my teachers it was hard for me to rock the boat or not be believed. I am not that nice or quiet anymore when it comes to these things. Though most teachers still liked having me they got a rude awakening when I had a problem with anything, with them or another student.

Chapter 11

Work, Work, Work

Everybody has bills. (I really wanted to start singing "Bitch Better Have My Money".) We all need to make money to live. And I'm guessing you're like most people who don't have generational money to live off of. So at some point, you're gonna need a job. To say that most entry-level jobs are not really good for our personalities and energy is an understatement. Because most are front-face customer work.

Honestly, everyone should work some kind of customer service job in their life. Maybe then we'll have fewer shitty people who treat people like crap.

Working With Customers

Especially when you start out working, there is not many options that doesn't require you to work with other people. Honestly, I think everyone should work customer service at least once. Maybe people would treat workers better if they had to be subjected to those awful people. Actually, see how hard the work is and how very little pay for it all.

And doing this work is a crash course in handling life in general. You can learn to let things go and how to keep your cool with ridiculous people. But it will also teach you how to stick up for yourself. Cause too many times the people that should (::cough:: management ::cough::) do not. To know that you do not deserve to be treated like crap. And it took me a couple of years to really find my balance of being good at my job and not being a doormat.

The peak of my IDGAF attitude was definitely in the eight horrible months I worked at a big blue box store. Management did not care about anyone. Fought to pay for an injury that they caused and did not want to give me accommodations. Not to mention the awful people that go there sometimes. I checked out when they wanted me to clean a self-check-out machine that a guy pleasured himself with.

Now, I hope no one ever has to go through with that to learn how to be professional and not let them know you think they are a POS. But I do have some tips to get you started.

Get Use To Smiling A Lot

Yeah, this really sucks especially since some of us get told this shit all the time. On one hand, you do this because it's expected of you in your interaction with customers. On the other, you will get some management that will remind you over and over. Wanting you to be "approachable" at all times, even if no is around. Which is really freaking frustrating but nothing you can do about it. The thing is you don't have to have a full smile. One way to look more "pleasant" is to make sure your mouth isn't turned down and have your eyebrows up just slightly.

Until you can train your face it will be hard to keep either of these up. Your face will be tired and sometimes hurt. But after a while, it will come naturally. Just like how you voice will change when how your normally talk to your 'customer service' voice.

Know Who You Can Trust

This goes for everyone at your job. You need to know what you can and cannot do with each person. Which manager doesn't mind some personal talk while you work. Which ones always want people moving? Which one will more likely change the schedule if you need it? Who will teach you new things? Then with the co-workers, you need to know who actually works and doesn't. Which ones can handle difficult people better. Who the teacher's pet is and who gossips. Whatever the whole dynamic of the place is.

There will be times you are going to need to vent about a customer. Some people will let you vent and bitch right along with you. Others will make you feel bad about it and want you to take the higher group. Since I didn't swear at them I think I'm doing good there. But also if something is bothering you know what manager will let you sit in the back for a bit to calm down. Or even let you take a quick break, on top of your regular ones.

But also you need to know who will help you if you have a problem customer. Someone who will back you up and believe you when you say you will not do a return. That we will not bend over backward because you are rude and don't deserve special treatment.

Hell, one of the bookstores I worked at like to have me be upfront at the registers when it was busy and there were a lot of new people there too. I could keep things moving along, help them with transactions that were not regular, and answer any questions. Also because I had no problem telling people no. And because I was very to the point I didn't get much arguing back. My tone was enough to show that that was the final answer.

Keep Your Answers Short

Trying too hard to explain things or be extra nice does not show confidence. If you are not confident then they will not believe you when you try to tell customers anything. You don't need to be clip about it, but you do not need to explain yourself. When you are in your job long enough you know what you are doing. If you do not know do not tell them an answer just because you think you should know it. Just ask someone else.

Being confident and not taking any crap will make things way easier. I honestly get a lot less crap from people because of this. Mostly because they can see I will not try to kiss ass, I will give the best service that is in my job requirements. Keep things short also shows that you will not engage in a debate with them over any of your policies. They are what they are.

Know The Return Policy Front and Back

We've all seen and heard stories of horrible customers and Karens out into the wild freaking out because they aren't getting what they want. It's usually when you're nervous and don't really know what you are doing that you scramble to answer their questions and tell them what you cannot do. And that is showing weakness. They will latch onto that and go for blood. They want their money back or something free. Whether or not something is actually wrong or within your power.

That way you can know right away if someone is going to argue with you are trying to trick you.

So know what exactly the return policy is for your job. And pay attention to all the little ways it can differ. Some managers can change things up or find workarounds. Actually know how the computer or register works so you can actually tell them it is literally impossible to do what they want. Someone can't return food for a new one because they said it wasn't cooked right and they ate more than half. Some things cannot be returned without a receipt, or a tag, or any way to show it actually came from your store. You cannot take something back three months later.

Have Something Specific You Are Good At

Now, this is kind of weird, but hear me out. I'm not saying go above and beyond they won't do it for you. But have a specific skill that is really helpful, either for the customer or coworker, that doesn't get needed very often. And sometimes you can't even plan for this, but definitely seize the opportunity if it pop-ups. It can be something you know always goes wrong with a specific order, a program, or just a specific regular customer.

Once I worked at a hotel running their cafe. And since it was a business hotel I had to be there really fucking early, literally get up at 3:30am early. But because I had worked at a Barnes and Noble before in their cafe that had most of the Starbucks drinks so I could mix the syrups they had to match the taste of drinks. Even made a recipe card for them. But my one big thing I was good at was making the drink for this one VIP. He was the only guy allowed to sell Waterford Crystals on TV. So he got flown to several different studios around the US every month. And I was the only person that he wanted to make his drink. It was very particular (but not hard) and I always got it right for him. And he always told all the managers how I always did it perfectly and he tipped me at least $20 each time.

I have worked at 3 different Barnes and Nobles over the years. So I was trained in a lot of things. Plus was there for so many different changes. One was that I was trained on their Nooks. Which they only did for a year or so. They do still sell them, but not as hard and they still have their app. So any time I go work at a different store I'm one of the only people that can troubleshoot things. I even knew more than most of the managers. So I got out of some tasks and projects just to help with that.

Pass It Off To Management

The best part about not being in charge? You can pass things on. Or course if it's within reason for you to do, but you got a Karen in the wild it's perfectly fine to pass them off to a manager. I can guarantee that you are not getting paid enough to deal with that shit.

And that is the part of the job of the manager or supervisor. They answer the questions you can't or handle people who need (or want) things that you personally cannot do. There are times when you will have incompetent or complete shits in the position, that's why you need to know who you can trust. Sometimes I just pass horrible people off to the shit ones just to be petty. They can't say anything because I usually do not have the authorization to do whatever it is.

In An Office

Working in an office has its own dynamics and culture different from customer service. There isn't much variety to the people you see. But some of those people can get a little too comfortable and nosy.

Speaking During Meetings

No one likes meetings. They last way too long. Most of them could just be an email. And there's always that one person who either won't shut up or keeps asking questions. It's just all too much. Even running my own business I still need to have them.

So we can avoid them. But there are ways to get better at them. To be able to actually get a word in and participate. Some of these are things you can do for yourself, others if you actually have a say in how the meetings are run.

- Plan ahead of time. Usually, you know that a meeting is going to happen at least a day in advance. So figure out what points need to be talked about. See what questions you could already have.
- Do not sit near the over-talker or the person who talks over people. Of course, this doesn't work if there are only 3 of you there or the room does not have space.

By sitting near them and you try to speak, it's not very hard for them to force the attention back to them. It's already mostly there. Don't make it easy for them to keep talking.

- Take notes. Part of this is to help remember what's actually being said. If you're too busy trying to figure out what to say and how to interject in you are missing some things. Another is so you will actually stay focused. If things go too fast, too far off-topic, or just too long we will zone out. Which will also lead into the third point, it makes you look like you're doing more when you are not. All that extra movement or writing, looking at a screen (computer, projector, etc), and then at the person is actually a non-verbal sign you are a part of the meeting. You are paying attention, without actually doing much to make it look like it.
- Choose your role in the beginning. This may seem a bit weird. But there are always certain roles in each meeting, especially in bigger ones. There's the Yes Mans, the questioners, someone who wants to give too much information, the help, and the one who moves things around. There are more, but these are the ones I see more. Of course, there are a few here no one wants to actually choose. I mostly take the mover role. Cause I want to keep the meeting going and done. But that works for my personality because my annoyance at still being there overrides me not wanting to talk.

Advocating For Yourself

Too many times we are not taught to advocate for ourselves. Mostly because our parents and do it for us or people think that its back-talking so don't want it to happen. There will always come a time where you will be treated bad and it will make you feel like shit.

Learning how to stand up for yourself, you will never be a bitch for doing it, will make sure you will stay happy in your work and life

Try To Align Goals With The Company's Goals

Of course, this doesn't mean you need to suck up to them and somehow make it 'seem' like what you are asking for is for their good too. Because you being taken care of as a worker is in their best good. But some companies are more focused on making more money and cutting costs. So knowing what the company wants and what they are building for and showing that what you are saying is the same.

You asking for more training, better communication, or even a shift anything will make it so you or even others are not wasting your time. Wasted time wastes their money.

Know Your Worth

Do not kiss ass just because you are scared that you will look bad for asking for anything. If they haven't fired you yet and there are no write-ups on your record then they want you there. Know that you do your job well and that you deserve respect (and better pay). Keep in mind that keep you is cheaper than finding a new person and having to train them.

Don't be a dick about it, but we rarely bring up anything that hasn't been bothering us for a while. And we just hold it in because we don't want to be a bother and no one else has brought it up yet. Then we notice other things that are wrong and make things not so easy. Until we see how much it's taking our time and energy. Which makes it harder to work.

Build Confidence

Before going in remember everything that you have already done and what you have learned from the job. Don't let the setbacks and frustrations cloud you that you are not good enough. The because you have to ask for help or tell someone something is wrong does not make you a bad worker or not a team player.

You haven't been fired yet and you're trying to give them a chance to be able to keep you. Loyalty should be both ways. It wastes their time and money to hire a new person and train them. But also remember that if they treat you like crap that you have every right to quit. Believe me, I know that it can be hard if you really need the job and there may not be options that you can see. But you have every right to try and make things better for yourself, which could also do the same for other coworkers.

Keep It Professional

It can be easy to get emotional when you are tired and feel like you are being taken advantage of. You can tell them how you are feeling but everything else needs to be about the facts. Show them what good work you do. Then show them how certain things are making you less productive. Or whatever ever you there for (a raise, trying to implement something new, reporting a co-worker) needs to be shown how it is costing them money. Because that is what managers and owners look at more. Whether or not they care about you, they care about making money and getting their work done with as little cost.

Go In With Ideas For How To Resolve and What Your Needs Are

Yeah, it's shitty to have to extra work, something that should be their job to figure out, but having a few solutions ready after you've told what your problem is will go a long way. It will also help them go in the direction you want to go. Maybe have something that would be great but not very likely to happen and something you want and isn't as hard to do. Then they see that your first option isn't so bad.

Have set ideas on what you want and need to happen, so if they try to negotiate you can be sure they get met and not just empty things that really don't help anyone but sounds good. If you want to make it so not everybody has to be a part of every single meeting, or every update turns into a meeting, you can give examples of why you and a co-worker don't need to be in the tech meeting when you do calls. Or for those who never have anything to do with some meetings can just get the notes from it emailed to them.

If you want to work from home 2 days a week you need to show that there are 2 days where you never take calls and there is only one meeting sometimes. By shifting a few things you all can save time and money. You would have more uninterrupted time and will email updates if your supervisor needs them. But after the pandemic there really isn't any excuse to say that a lot of people could not work some of the time at home, they made it work before.

Running Your Own Business and Being A Boss

For some of us running our own business is a dream. We can choose our own schedule and decide how much interaction we have with people. I built mine for the lifestyle that I wanted. Working from home, creative, product and content base, freedom to choose my schedule, and no one around me. I could have easily done a service business, even had a few services in the beginning. But it's not what I wanted and just didn't bring me any joy to do.

This only works for those who are self-starters and can work independently. Even though we as introverts would rather be left alone for a lot of things, that doesn't always translate to work. Some people do not want to be in charge, at all. Some would rather have set tasks and time to do things. Others really just want to do something a little mindless and leave it there to go home.

Sometimes You're Alone Too Much

I know, this might seem weird but you can have too much time alone. One of the best things about running a business is building to your wants and needs. That's what I did. I do some events but mostly work from home. My freelance work only has a couple of emails a week. I mostly make products and rarely have to handle customers. I have several podcasts but I get to schedule when I talk to people. Plus I decide who it is and I have them on because they are teaching something important and telling a great story. Wins all around there.

But then everything else I do is alone. My writing, editing, marketing, and all the back-end for my business. Which I do love, don't get me wrong, but at times even I'm tired of seeing the same screen and walls. Even I can see that I talk to my dog way too much.

Hiring Help and Actually Being In Charge

Oh boy, this is anxiety-inducing. Especially if you've never really been in charge of anything big. because this is everything and all about your livelihood. We have no problem doing all the things alone. It's part of the appeal, but at some point to grow more you need others to take things off your plate so you can work more on the money-making part.

This gives me flashbacks to high school doing school projects with people who always talked over people. Thinking they're in charge just because they are louder. Not always being the one who knows what the hell they are doing or the smarter one (most in my experience were not very smart). Too many times doing more of the work than you were supposed to and the others making it you should be grateful to be in their group. Which is all shit.

So it can take us way too long to actually hire someone to help. On one hand, because we are dictated to more often than not. We know we can get things done and it can be so hard to explain to others even if they try to help. On the other hand, we don't get much experience with being in charge. On teaching others how to do things our way. To being ok with doing it our way and not feel pressured to change just because someone else doesn't like it. And we are not promoted to any kind of management roles often when we do start working.

Just like everything else in life we're just going to have to push through it. If you want to make your business thrive and actually make a full-time living you will have to be a boss. Get comfortable with training people, give orders, and telling people they did something wrong. You will also have to take care of customers. Whether or not you do a service or products. Because all of that will happen and it will up to you to take care of it.

You can build it, however, your want but you really can't avoid people altogether. Though there is freelance work you can do where you only communicate through email and chat. And that was great for me for a while. Mostly because I didn't have set hours to work and could work on my business part-time in the beginning. It also trained me to work more efficiently on my own, manage my time, as well as set up boundaries.

Standard Operating Procedure

This is such a lifesaver when you have to do things with other people, whether it's actual employees or contract workers. I know it can seem scary with its big corporate lingo. But it's just very specific instructions on how you do something.

It can be as detailed as you want, but I would try to get enough that someone who read it could reasonably understand it. It's literally the steps you take, how you do it, and any programs and links you use in the process. And you need to do it for everything you do. I mean everything. I don't care if its time consuming, it will help you in the long run. It needs to clear enough that anyone can work from it still get the same results.

First, it gives you a place to have all your information to look back on. Especially for things that you need to do in your business but doesn't happen even weekly. I don't remember most of my accounting stuff off the top of my head because I only do it once a month. Even though I've been doing it every month for the last 4 years. Writing it out can also show you where you repeat things or can take steps out. It also can show you where you can move things around to make everything operate quicker.

But then, when you do get the help you don't have to figure out how to tell the person how to do the thing, what things they will need to get it done, or what parts you need to do before they can do their part. The groundwork was already done. I get help from a graphic designer to do all my social media graphics for all my podcasts. So I need to know what the title of the episodes are and what order they go in. Plus if it's an interview the info for them. I also need to have a timeline so I know how many she needs to make in a month so I can stay ahead.

You can just have them in your Google Docs so they can be easily shared. I even have them saved to different folders so I can have related files together. Like examples of the graphics I like. My logos and whole brand identify. Other instructions on how to get into different programs and what their logins are.

Chapter 12

Travel The World

Traveling is one of the greatest things you can do for yourself. It opens your mind and world to everything the world has to offer. You see so many wonders out there, different cultures, and ways of being. For many it's also the only time when they completely relax for an extended period of time.

There are all kinds of ways to travel and though some parts can be good for introverts, it doesn't always translate for the whole trip. Yeah, I am great for long periods of time just reading or listening to music. But personally, I don't care to travel for days just to get somewhere. When I was in my teens and 20s it was fun and cool. Plus I didn't have the money sometimes to pay for a plane ticket. Now I'd rather spend more time being where I need to be and exploring there. I don't have as much patience for cross-country drives.

Solo

I believe that everyone should travel alone at least once in their life. It pushes your limits. You get to decide everything that you do. And you notice so much more. You have to rely on yourself for everything, especially your enjoyment.

I mean, some of them I hardly talked to anyone and it was glorious. I walked everywhere and took pictures, hiked, and ate whatever I wanted. There was no one to work with or have to placate if you do something they don't want to do. Most people are not early birds like me, but when I'm traveling I will get up before the ass crack of dawn just to get sunrise photos. And I could do that every morning.

There is such a stigma for doing really anything alone. Like you don't have any friends to do anything with you. Or that you are some weirdo or psycho. Then there's the fear for your safety, which is a valid thing to worry about. I had to wait while I was abroad to tell my mom about my travels. It gave her anxiety because for more of them I did travel alone. Not only was I out of the country for a long period of time but she could not help me if I really needed something with any speed.

So there are some general tips to always do when you are traveling (especially abroad):

- Search for dangers in the area. This can be looking up news articles, travel blogs, or check the State Department's website for country updates and enroll in the Smart Traveler Enrollment Program (STEP). Know what the most common crime is there. Know the area inside and out, like safe places to go or an Embassy.

- Make copies of important documents. That's your driver's license, passport, hotel reservations, plane ticket reservations, directions to places. And have physical and digital copies of everything. Hell, I even have a spare phone with me just so I can have a backup and be able to wipe my main phone if it gets stolen.
- Make sure friends and family know your plans. They get a copy of everything as well. Have set days and times that you touch base with people. Find where they need to call if they think something is wrong; the hotel, police, or whatever.
- Don't draw attention. Seriously, leave most of your fancy stuff at home. Have a few things if you are going to somewhere fancy for dinner or something, but only a few. I've heard some women have cheaper wedding rings that they wear while traveling so it wouldn't be as bad if they got robbed. You don't need to flaunt having any money.
- Be wary of public Wi-Fi. Especially abroad. They know when there are foreigners using it and can quickly get into your devices and steal things. Honestly, it can be less safe than in the States, but really you don't need to be on the internet when out traveling much.
- Be aware of your surroundings. Do not look like you are lost. Don't make it easy for people to spot you as alone and ignorant. Pay attention if someone is following you. Don't be too forthcoming about what you are doing or who you are with.
- Safeguard your hotel room. This is where you will keep most of your valuables and sleep. Don't let the cleaning service come often. Then someone knows when you are not in your room, plus it's better for

the environment. In the nicer hotels use the safe. I've even brought a bike lock with me so I could lock my luggage to something that was bolted down. Thieves rarely have bolt cutters when stealing from rooms. Also, have a good lock for your luggage.

A side note about keeping yourself safe is when you travel with an expensive camera to have a cord that is connected to you. Same with a bag or purse. I have a small retractable cord that wrapped around my belt and around a metal loop on my bag. It's very common for thieves to run up behind you or drive up on a scooter, cut the strap, and run off. Had that happen to me in Athens, but they just wrenched their arm and fell on their face.

With Another Person

You would think going with one other person would be the best option. It's not a crown and you should like the person enough to want to travel with them. Fewer opinions and more likely to compromise on things. Which can and cannot be the truth. You can have a great time with them and the whole experience can be better with them there.

A trip is something that's not normal, everyday life. And the person you love and care about may change into someone different when on a vacation. They may not be used to making so many decisions on taking care of things on their own. They may be anxious about new things. Or they could want to be pampered and expect everything to be done for them. The worst part is these things may not show up until after you left, when you are stuck with them.

Years ago I went on vacation with my family. My parents stayed a week longer than me and my brother. He had to get back for work and I had college. But at that point I had a lot more traveling experience than him. He is also a nervous flyer so I had everything. Had the plane tickets, made sure we were at the right gate, and answer any questions. From security.

See not only was he a nervous flyer he had a big beard, wore an Afghan scarf, and basically looked like a lighter skin Middle Eastern man. This was well within the same decade of 9/11 and my brother is an idealist. Believing that he shouldn't get "randomly selection" out of principle of racial profiling. Now, I believe in the same principle but knew him not changing anything so he would look a little less like peoples' fear at an airport was going to give up problems.

And surprise, surprise he got stopped at every airport to be checked. All but one several times. On the way to the gate, whenever he left to get food, on his way back again. Japan it only happened once and that was because after he got checked getting off the plane they told him he should just stay at his gate and no one would bother him. They even followed behind us for a bit waving others off so we could just get there. I had to walk around to get food for both of us. He was annoyed by this and I had no sympathy.

This is an extreme example and luckily most trips won't have this problem. But there are some things you can work on before you go to make sure things go more smoothly.

- Make sure who will pay for what and what the division is of costs
- Make a list of things you both want to do and make a plan (even just a loose one) of what you can and can-

not fit into the trip. Making sure you both get some things you both want to do.

· Do not pack your days full. You will not be wasting time by allowing rest. I'd be madder to not remember half the trip because I was exhausted and overwhelmed.

· Do no spend every moment together. Less likely to hate each other by the end. And make sure you let them know this is in the plans before. I'm usually a way more early bird than anyone else. So a lot of the time I will get up before dawn to walk and do photography. Or when the other person is not a morning person at all I leave to have breakfast by myself and they can wake at their leisure (and less cranky).

Do not lose a good relationship over this. Remember how your relationship works in everyday life. What little things bother or annoy you about each other. Don't think because it's a different situation that things will be different.

With A Group

When we go places it can be fun to go with others. But only if you plan for your energy. The more people mean more opinions, the more people to please. And when there's a range of ages and "status" in life there will be some who want to have more say. This can be going with family, parents usually having more of a say no matter what. Or friends who are more well off or going someplace they've already been to.

So you need to figure out what you want to get out of the trip and talk to the people you are going with to see where they stand. First, so people can know what everyone wants. But also to set boundaries on how much time you all are spending together. Some people just assume that everyone will be doing everything together. Or will want to tag along if you go off to do something different.

And if there are kids coming, that changes the whole dynamic. Depending on the kids and parents and how others deal with kids is a whole nother ball game. Some will want their kids to be able to do everything with everyone. Some will cater everything to them. Or worse, they'll expect others to watch their kids so they can "have a break". Not caring that you are also there to relax, not to be a free babysitter.

With Friends

This should be fun for you. Hopefully, you actually like these people or can at least tolerate them. Other people that you wouldn't have chosen may have been invited. Your significant other's friend and girlfriend, another friend's close friend, or even you could be the odd one in the group.

One of the bigger problems is actually not getting left out of things. Sometimes because you may not get along with everyone and don't care to do something they want to can get them use to not including you in things. You should be having fun with them and they should want to include you in things as well. It should all be fun and relaxing. Supposedly be less stress than with family, but some people can change on vacation, like going with just one other person.

With Family

This is a minefield in itself. Family dynamics are always tricky to manage. Especially when you're the kid, no matter if you are an adult now. Your own parents and other family members can find it hard to treat you like an adult when they've known you since you were in diapers. And some are too use to being in charge to give up any control, in any way.

Under no circumstances do you give your money to anyone else. You pay for what you say you will pay for. Make sure you have your own room, no sharing (at least for most of the trip). Have your own key and some way to get around on your own. Do not let someone else pack all your time with activities. Even if you have to get one other member to go do something different with you. Keep some kind of control and freedom.

Definitely make sure you have a lot of music, movies, and shows downloaded onto devices. You never know what internet will be available where you are and for your own sanity, you will need to be able to drown them out sometimes. I brought backup battery chargers so I could use things almost constantly if need be.

If you need to sneak away for some quiet, do it. It shouldn't be too hard to figure out everyone's habits and quirks. There are always times that you can just slip out and be a block away before anyone notices. Or be the one who volunteers to pick something up...and take your time getting back.

Chapter 13

How To Avoid People

Not gonna lie, I made an episode about this, and it's the most talked about for my listeners. Half because people found it funny, but the other half saying they've done some of the same things.

We've all wanted to avoid someone. Out on the street. In the classroom or at work. Hell, I've avoided family at big gatherings because I just didn't want to have to answer the same damn question every single time I see them. Sometimes we just don't want to talk to people.

The biggest thing to always keep in mind about avoiding people is the level of embarrassment you are willing to live with. Embarrassment if you get caught trying to avoid them. But mostly in what you are willing to do to get away. Cause other people will see you, sometimes your own friends and family. Now I have a pretty high threshold. Some people have had more second-hand embarrassment than I do doing it. I have climbed out of windows, dropped to the ground, and crawled under tables. If there was a way to get out of interacting without them knowing, I'd do it.

I like to break them down into three parts. The first is the easiest because you can get away with doing them most of the time and can explain it away easily too. The second only works if you are a little quick on your feet and only with some embarrassment. The third is hard. You need to be, at least in the moment, to not care at all about others' opting on of you. Because some people will look at you weird if not outright tell you what you did was wrong. Though, only if they see or you tell them.

Not gonna lie, I've only heard two other people who have done things like this as me. How many people have you known to hide from a guy who tried to confess to you but said a bunch of random and sometimes flowery things you had no idea what he was saying then walks away? To start following you until you had to ask him to leave you alone. Then his friends had to tell you he thought since I didn't outright reject him, even though I wasn't given the chance, we were together. And he was telling everyone who would listen that I was going to visit his mom with him soon.

I noped out of that quick. One time jumped through my friend's window so he wouldn't see me. But he knew she lived there and went there to look for me. I dropped to the floor and army crawled to her roommate's room and climbed out his window. I just didn't care.

Now, I know this isn't a specific incident that is about being an introvert. But this is an example of the lengths I would go. But any interaction with him always became a spectacle since all the guys thought it was so funny.

Level 1

"Please don't disturb me." This could be playing on your phone, or even just pretending to be on your phone, such as playing games, social media, and texting. It could also be having headphones on and listening to music, or pretending to do so. You can also be reading, but that doesn't always work because people assume you're not doing anything important and interrupt you anyway. Sometimes I will read with headphones on. Some other ideas include studying or working, whether it is for real or fake. Some people won't respect that you want to be left alone though.

Sadly, this doesn't work on all people. Some will just not take the hint or think what they want is more important than what you are doing. You have several options when this happens. You can be nice and see what they want and hopefully it's something quick and actually not intrusive. You could go to Level 2 which isn't as nice. Or you can go straight to not being nice at all.

Some people may not be comfortable being not nice, especially as a female with our training with always being nice, helpful, and accommodating.

Level 2

"Leave me alone" level. It's a little less nice and can be passive-aggressive. Some options are turning your music up a lot louder in your headphones so others can hear it, changing your route to avoid someone, faking a call on your phone, or going to the bathroom and taking your time to do your makeup or saying there was a long line.

Another idea is staring off into the distance and zoning out with unfocused eyes. You may realize someone is waving at you off in the distance, but try not to react, look vaguely in their area, and then move your line of sight slowly like you are distracted by a bird or something. Sometimes this doesn't work as well. You kind of have to be a good actor or liar.

Level 3

This is more extreme. Use this level if you get caught or seen. Sometimes it is necessary and there isn't a way to avoid being kind of rude. You can literally drop out of sight, jump out of places such as windows, pretend you misunderstand or mishear things, disappear around the corner and making a run for it, or act weird or crazy on purpose so people leave you alone.

Years ago I helped a friend dodge her ex's mom. He was abusive and she couldn't believe her precious baby could do any of those things. So the mother went straight to attacking my friend since she had to be a lying, jealous whore. One day we see her in the same walkway at the mall. She sees her but isn't quite sure since we're a ways away. I not so subtly walk into my friend, pushing her into the nearest store. The mom looks into the store when she got closer but I just pushed my friend to the back of the store and kept an eye out until she left.

I have climbed out of second-story windows, crawled under cars, and created a distraction when the person was trying to talk to me so I could get away. Most people would not get to this level. They either get too embarrassed or it would never cross their mind to do any of these options.

Different Mindset

It takes a different kind of mindset to be comfortable to avoid people. You need to be good with possibly getting caught. Some people get embarrassed easily, especially if other people are possibly watching. So you need to know what level you want to be at. Not what's easy. Because there are times you do not want to do the nice thing. There are people who do not deserve your time or are actually pretty toxic.

And it can feel wrong to do some of these things. To some it's mean, others downright dishonest. There are some who see the world as very black and white and want you to feel guilty for doing any of these. I say it's up to you and your conscience. It's your time and peace of mind.

For me, I've done all three levels and have no shame for it. I've even told people some of the things I've done to get away. I know perfectly well how some people view me in a not-so-good light after that. That just shows me they are not my people. And they most likely don't get my humor. Or that they do not respect other's boundaries.

Boundaries For The Rest Of The World

Having your own boundaries and trying to live them healthily is very important. But sometimes we can get so caught up in them that we don't realize we are holding on to them so strongly. That some people may need to be reminded and given examples, given time to adjust themselves. Not everyone is out there trying to get around them. Though we all hear so many stories of people purposefully doing that.

If you do actually like the person you can't always avoid them each time you don't want to deal with them. Sooner or later they will catch on, on their own or someone will tell them. And if you do not actually bring whatever you are avoiding up with them then they may stop talking to you. That is a possible consequence for avoiding people. Sooner or later you will get caught and it will hurt someone's feelings.

If it is someone you want very little to do with or is very rude when they have you alone then it is fine to do. But if it's someone you care about then you do need to talk to them about why you avoid them. You don't use this stuff willy nilly. They are mostly for mosey strangers or the people take up too much of your time, don't respect you, or are awful people.

You also need to respect other people's boundaries. Respect goes both ways, we don't get a pass just because we don't want to interact with people as much. And we should all be good advocates for everyone to get their wants and needs met and feel safe with us. Sometimes what we set up will actually clash with another's boundaries. It doesn't happen very often but it does. You can either work around what you can with each other and make some adjustments (for the both of you, not you just to make them comfortable) or you two just don't interact. And either option is equally valid.

Chapter 14

Getting Through Certain Situations

Sadly, we get into situations we don't want to.... which is mostly shit we gotta do every day. I'm only half kidding. We actually enjoy our friends and family and they want to do things that require a lot more people. These are the situations that most of us will have to go through, multiples times. And sometimes you will have to be around people you don't know or even like, but you need to make an appearance. Others are just things we go through in life.

Weddings

Now, I have a huge family. No lie, both my parents have 7 brothers and sisters and countless aunts, uncles, and cousins. So I've been to my fair share of nuptials. And for the most part, I've actually enjoyed going to them. Not so much when I was younger and it was for a friend because

I would know no one there. So I have found some ways to make them less awkward and boring.

- Get there early. You'll have a better chance of talking to the couple and a few other key people before it gets too busy. Which means you can also leave early, and part of that time was when there was no crowd.
- Explore the area. It's easy to get bored when there's no one to talk to. So just wander around. Find all the bathrooms, check out all the rooms, the grounds outside. One time the wedding was at a community center and at the other side was a basketball game so I sat and watched for a while trust to kill time.
- Find a task to do. Another good reason to get there early is that you can see if help is needed. Its passes the time quicker. People will talk to you more after seeing you help. Plus more people will remember you so no one can say that you didn't go. Seriously, as a middle school kid, I pumped the keg for half the night. Don't worry the cop there said as long as I didn't pore it or touch any drinks I was fine.
- Sneak in some entertainment. Bring headphones, a game boy, or a book. It's easier now since everyone has phones now. But the best thing to do is not right where everyone is. That partially why you do some exploring, to find a place to hide for a while. But you have to keep making an appearance throughout to make sure people don't think you left or got kidnapped.

Living alone

Now, this isn't really something you don't want to do. Some of us may not get the chance to live on our own having to stay at our parents' longer, living with roommates or our significant others. So I thought I go over some tips and tricks to make it easier and safer.

- Check everything when moving in. Check all vents and look for any hides holes. Anything that can have a camera in it. Make sure the place is actually empty. Replace anything that seems hinky. change the screws in doors, locks, and windows, especially in rentals. The ones they usually put in won't hold up to a kick to the door.
- Get a pet. Only if you want one and will actually take care of it. Mostly any pet that doesn't live in a cage. Dogs are best because many people will think twice, but cats can be a deterrent too. They are also great companions.
- Add extra security. I know we all can't afford a building with a doorman or building security so you need to add in your own. This can be changing the locks or adding extras. Having cameras set up. Even having a system with trusted people for you to send out a quick SOS.
- Get to know neighbors. This is adding security because you can look out for each other's. But also so you can know who the problem people are in the area.

Conferences

Not gonna lie, I love conferences. Yeah, there's a lot of people but I actually don't have to talk to most of them. Even when I go to one where I know a lot of people there are plenty of opportunities to get away. What people don't get is that there are not many conferences happening in a year. So they are really spread out. At most I've gone to five in a year.

It might be a little different for others who have to go for work-related things. But all the ones I've gone to have been to topics I really enjoy. Podcasting, blogging, business, anime, wolves, pets, and green living just to name a few. But even if you are wanting to be there there are some tips you can do to make it easier and more likely you'll last until the end. Especially if it's several days long.

- Make your own schedule. Most of these things will have the full schedule up on their website before it happens. So look through to see what things you want to go to and find the times where you can skip. There will always be a time where you're not really excited about anything. These are also the better times to get food and go to the bathroom.
- Bring a friend. You don't always have to go alone. Have someone that will keep you comfortable and rescue you from horrible conversations. Of course, make sure you two aren't stuck at the hip the whole time. But having someone you trust there (and maybe less introverted than you?) can help you open up more. Just make sure you're still open to talking to others.

- Find all the secluded areas. Check out a map, ask the front desk, or just take a walk around the venue. Figure out where the majority of the conference will be or if there are other events happening at the same time. Then see where there are pockets where you can find some quiet. A lot of hotels have sitting areas littered throughout. They will also have some outside. Smoking areas, near elevators, and amenities. Find where all the bathrooms are. Not only will it take you away from the noise of the main area, women's restroom lines can be pretty long.
- Stay in the same building or really close. If it's more than a day-long try to stay where everything is. You will have more time to sleep in and have your own private place to be alone. Hell, even your own bathroom.
- Leave when you can. They usually make it you can get everything you need right at the conference, but sometimes it's just better to get out for a bit. If you made some friends suggest going to a restaurant to eat for dinner. Off to do a coffee run for people. Go for a morning walk before everything starts.

Group Projects

The dreaded group project. The bane of any introvert's school life. Sadly they don't really go away in a work setting either. I'm not sure if it was worse when you were the smarter kid or the one who needed more help. Either way trying to decide by committee, divvying up work, and getting the one lazy ass to actually do something makes it all awful.

I already went over some of this in chapter School Life. But sadly, in too many situations you can't get away from them. A lot of different jobs have people working in groups. A lot of different social groups or hobbies do them sometimes. And the same people you had a problem with before don't really change as adults. If they were useless then, they're useless now. And your boss will be less likely to make sure everyone is doing their work or won't care if someone takes credit or steals from another.

The best thing to do is to keep a trail for yourself. Make divvying up work and tasks get put in writing, especially email. I don't care if tryout working with your best friends that your love and trust. People will forget things and this will cut off any chance of fights or anyone accusing you of lying or being lazy.

Also make sure you keep higher-ups in the loop. Even if it's just a quick question with a leader or manager. And just sliding in most of what you are doing and what some of the others are doing too. Even if you already know the answer. And make sure the others know you talked to them. That will be a small deterrent that they can't hide behind only a few people knowing what's going on. Another thing is to CC anybody else in those emails.

So if anything goes wrong or someone is trying to throw you under the bus you have receipts of what was said and agreed upon. And do not worry about seeming mean. This is your work and you could lose out on promotions or even lose your job if you don't protect yourself. There is a difference between being nice and kind. Kind is superficial. Kindness is about everyone, including yourself.

Conflict

I went over part of this in the Boundaries chapter, but it gets harder. We will have these in many different ways with many people throughout our lives. And in order to not be a doormat, you need to find your own way to face it. People will disagree or misunderstand you. Some purposefully. Half of it is knowing what you can handle and how you will react, the other half is having enough self-confidence and self-respect to execute it.

The problem being is that you are different. So others will think they are right because they are louder, or seem more confident, or is more charismatic. It can be hard to articulate our thoughts and feelings on the spot, also when it's tense and awkward. But if we avoid it then things don't get resolved and we can get walked over because we just let things slide.

It takes much more energy to actively ignore your problems than to address them directly. Yet people often do exactly that because they're afraid of entering an uncomfortable situation or inconveniencing someone. That means people and situations are taking up a lot of your time and energy. Constantly living with a roommate who plays loud music all the time. Always letting people borrow your car. Helping out at a friend's to clean up.

But by not avoiding it it will make you set and protect your boundaries. You also get more out of your relationships. Especially friendships you should be able to be open and honest with them. They will never know something is bothering you if you don't say anything, so cannot change for the better for your friendship. You can also better see if they are actually good friends if they respect your boundaries.

There are some other small things you can do to help you handle conflict:

- Normalize Your Own Feelings
- Shake Your Jitters Out
- Plan to Speak Up
- Own Your Strengths
- Accept Yourself Regardless of the Outcome

It doesn't always have to be about hurting others or always winning, but you can't be a doormat. You deserve to be treated with respect just like everyone else. You don't need to be loud and make it a spectacle in front of everyone.

Chapter 15

Sendoff

Wanting better things in life you really shouldn't be too hard. But some people really can't leave others alone. But that isn't your problem. You do you bo. We all can live a fun and fulfilling lives just the way we are. Nothing is wrong with us and we are not "difficult" for being outside the norm.

Everyone has the right to want to arrange their lives to make things easier. All the tips and tricks I've given would not be side-eyed if it wasn't associated with being an introvert. I am perfectly happy with being one. It has not lessened anything in my life, it just makes me different. Which we all are because we are all living beings with depths. It would all be boring if we all were actually the same like society tries to push.

We are all growing up not knowing what to do. So just do what's right for you. It really isn't hard for all of us to live in the world together. Growing up is never easy anyways. We have to go through puberty and the influx of emotions and hormones. Try to figure out who we are and what we want to do with our lives. Figure out how we are going to live, which is already hard with education and the cost of living skyrocketing everywhere. Jobs paying crap and adding more work.

So every little thing we can do to make things easy is just fine. Every body does it in their own way. People move to be in better school districts. Buy cars with better gas mileage for their long commutes.

Most of this is not very serious and can be fun along the way. It's all working on ourselves because we can't change how others think or behave. We can just take care of ourselves and hope to find other like-mind people to share our space with. We are stuck with ourselves. No one else in the world will be with us and have to hear our thoughts more. So we need to get comfy and happy with who we are.

Our relationships and the things we go through in life can be improved and there's nothing wrong with that. The difference is to upgrade parts of you and not hating who you are fundamentally. Only one can actually be changed. And I'm not gonna waste time and energy on a futile thing. Wouldn't you rather enjoy your life?

I hope this book gave you enough courage to create change in your life so you can have your own space in the world. Not just the space that is given to you. You can live loud and proud just by living quietly. Breaking your own confines is an act of rebellion. And have fun with it all.

Let them be mad you're enjoying life.

Appendix

Intro

Vilay, Anung. *Living Off The Hustle*. Courageous Creativity, 2021.

Vilay, Anung. *The Introvert's Bubble*. Courageous Creativity. 2017-present Courageouscreativity.co/podcast

Vilay, Anung. *I Don't Wanna Fit In*. Courageous Creativity. 2020-present Courageouscreativity.co/podcast

Cain, Susan. *Quiet: The Power of Introverts in a World That Can't Stop Talking*. New York: Broadway Paperbacks, 2013. Print.

Recharging

https://www.themarysue.com/watching-tv-is-good-for-you/

https://greatergood.berkeley.edu/article/item/how_journaling_can_help_you_in_hard_times

Being Yourself

Duffield-Thomas, Denise. *Chillpreneur: The New Rules for Creating Success, Freedom, and Abundance on Your Terms*. Hay House Business. 2020

Setting Boundaries

Morningstar, Dana. *Out of the Fog: Moving From Confusion to Clarity After Narcissistic Abuse.* Morningstar Media. 2017

Romance

Hall, Jeffrey A. *Five flirting styles.* Don Mills, Ontario, Canada : Harlequin, 2013

Anung is the owner and mastermind behind Courageous Creativity. Which started as a side hustle and turned into a full business by combining a bunch of hustles together. Loves helping others work on their mindset and what's possible with money to fellow misfits and black sheep.

She is also the host of The Introvert's Bubble and I Don't Wanna Fit In podcasts, with more to come. Second half of Podcast du Nord, podcasting conference and learning. Serial starter and dreamer.

She lives in Minnesota with her dog and coworker Enzo. Who has won Employee of the Month for years somehow. Constantly reading, writing, and creating, plus talking to other creatives.

CPSIA information can be obtained
at www.ICGtesting.com
Printed in the USA
BVHW041746200721
612410BV00016B/1273

9 781736 300848